Evolution of the Global Fitness Industry

The pandemic has taught us all how important it can be to look after our physical and mental health, and how worthwhile it is to invest in taking care of ourselves. This short book illustrates the main trends that are modifying the fitness industry worldwide and highlights contemporary relevance to strategic change. It outlines what is currently happening within the promising fitness market and analyses the major emerging trends and the scientific data, referring to startups that could become very interesting market players in the years to come. Sustainability and technology will be the subject of in-depth analysis, as they represent the main drivers that will guide the sector in the future. The book also considers the most important aspect of sustainability related to the fitness industry and wellness more generally: the Silver Economy. The analysis is supported by an extensive database involving the 100 leading companies in the sector worldwide. The novelty of this research is to provide a document analysing the typical characteristics of this market, consumption dynamics, consumer triggers, and underlying the socio-economic scenario. The treatment of key themes such as fitness-tech startups, sport strategic management and above all innovation and sustainability make the book unique and appealing to researchers, academics, students, and practitioners.

Patrizia Gazzola is a Professor of Management, Business Combination and Business Planning in the Department of Economics at the University of Insubria, Varese, Italy.

Enrica Pavione is an Aggregate Professor of Business Management in the Department of Economics at the University of Insubria, Varese, Italy.

Francesco Ferrazzano is a Researcher in the field of Business, specifically in the Fitness Industry, in Italy.

Routledge Focus on Business and Management

The fields of business and management have grown exponentially as areas of research and education. This growth presents challenges for readers trying to keep up with the latest important insights. *Routledge Focus on Business and Management* presents small books on big topics and how they intersect with the world of business research.

Individually, each title in the series provides coverage of a key academic topic, whilst collectively, the series forms a comprehensive collection across the business disciplines.

Leadership and Strategic Management
Decision-Making in Times of Change
Paolo Boccardelli and Federica Brunetta

Artificial Intelligence and Project Management
An Integrated Approach to Knowledge-Based Evaluation
Tadeusz A. Grzeszczyk

Organizational Aesthetics
Artful Visual Representations of Business and Organizations
Barbara Fryzel and Aleksander Marcinkowski

Open Strategy for Digital Business
Managing in ICT-Driven Environments
Ewa Lechman, Joanna Radomska and Ewa Stańczyk-Hugiet

Purpose-driven Innovation Leadership for Sustainable Development
A Qualitative Case Study Approach
Gaia Grant

Evolution of the Global Fitness Industry
Strategy, Sustainability and Innovation
Patrizia Gazzola, Enrica Pavione and Francesco Ferrazzano

For more information about this series, please visit: www.routledge.com/Routledge-Focus-on-Business-and-Management/book-series/FBM

Evolution of the Global Fitness Industry

Strategy, Sustainability and Innovation

Patrizia Gazzola, Enrica Pavione and Francesco Ferrazzano

NEW YORK AND LONDON

First published 2025
by Routledge
605 Third Avenue, New York, NY 10158

and by Routledge
4 Park Square, Milton Park, Abingdon, Oxon, OX14 4RN

Routledge is an imprint of the Taylor & Francis Group, an informa business

ISBN: 978-1-032-75588-5 (hbk)
ISBN: 978-1-032-75793-3 (pbk)
ISBN: 978-1-003-47569-9 (ebk)

DOI: 10.4324/9781003475699

Typeset in Times New Roman
by codeMantra

Contents

Figures

Introduction

The book outlines the current situation in the promising fitness market, analyzing the main emerging trends worldwide and the economic data of startups that could become very interesting market players in the years to come. Medical News Today defines fitness as the ability to perform daily tasks with optimal performance, endurance, and strength by managing illness, fatigue, and stress, and the reduction of sedentary behavior. As can be seen from the definition, the concept of fitness is not just limited to a competitive environment, such as the practice of competitive or professional sports. On the contrary, fitness pertains to all individuals, some more and some less, and is a fundamental part of their lives.

The fitness industry has undergone major changes in recent years, both on the demand and supply sides. The recent pandemic has taught everyone how important it is to take care of our physical and mental health and how much it is worth spending to take care of ourselves. For this reason, it is expected that as people's spending power increases, so will their purchases related to fitness and wellness more generally. On the supply side, the main drivers that are moving the sector forward are the search for sustainable approaches and innovation, which are leading the fitness world to create original business models. In light of these considerations, this book explores the main trends that characterize the sector, starting from an overall overview of the sector's weight in the economy. The main changes on the demand side are then analyzed, and attention is focused on the drivers that drive modern companies, first and foremost, sustainability and innovation. Last but not least, the final part of the book is experimental, comprising two different levels of analysis. We created a questionnaire that is useful for doing this type of analysis, not only in this sector but in other types of business and innovation research. We checked 100 specific startups in this sector by analyzing each one's website to understand its message, or what the company wants to convey through its main space. The 100 companies were selected based on the following criteria: availability of a website, geographical area, primary focus on fitness, and degree of notoriety gained over time. Starting from these premises, the book is structured in seven chapters.

DOI: 10.4324/9781003475699-1

Chapter 1 frames the world of fitness by offering an overview of industry data and analysis globally, outlining the current state of the promising fitness market. Chapter 2 explores the main trends in demand by identifying the different types of consumers and their needs. The various types of modern consumers are described, focusing attention on two phenomena adjacent to fitness, namely personalized nutrition and sleep quality. Chapter 3 focuses on the traditional drivers that characterize the fitness industry, i.e., funding sources and emerging business models. Chapters 4 and 5 analyze the drivers of the future, which are already driving the sector today: sustainability and technology. These two factors can be understood as key to effectively interpreting the phenomenon of fitness-tech startups and their evolution worldwide. This is a relevant topic, as the innovative drivers in the fitness industry are constantly evolving and the future of fitness seems to highlight promising developments that will result in new and original business models. In particular, Chapter 4 explores the theme of the silver economy and addresses its importance in modern societies. In Chapter 6, we review the survey that was developed to investigate the four drivers of new fitness startups. Finally, Chapter 7 details our extensive empirical investigation, focused on a sample of 100 startups in the fitness world, with the aim of investigating the dynamics of the sector and development prospects in light of the drivers identified in the previous analysis.

1 The evolution of the Global Fitness Industry

1.1 Introduction

The concept of fitness falls under the broader definition of wellness, described in the 1960s as "an integrated method of functioning aimed at maximizing the potential of which the individual is capable" (Dunn, 1961). This definition, which emphasizes individual commitment from a certain starting point within a hierarchy of health possibilities, remains relevant today. Subsequent theoretical contributions have referred to this definition but emphasized the individualistic character of wellness, seen as "self-responsibility, nutritional awareness, physical fitness, stress management, and environmental sensitivity" (Ardell, 1982). Definitions of wellness have continued to vary somewhat, but they have always considered Ardell's five dimensions to cover vast areas of personal and social life. The Berkeley Wellness Letter defines wellness as "optimal physical, mental, and emotional well-being, a preventative way of living that reduces — sometimes even eliminates — the need for remedies. It emphasizes personal responsibility in making the life choices and self-care decisions that will improve quality of life" (BerkeleyWellness.com, 2013). Health promotion and optimal health are often used interchangeably with wellness, as in Michael O'Donnell's (2009) definition of optimal health as "dynamic balance of physical, emotional, social, spiritual, and intellectual health". In relatively recent times, indicators have been developed to measure the state of well-being; Gallup, for example, looking at a significant sample of American citizens each year, measures well-being using the Healthways Well-Being Index Composite Score, evaluating six domains: life assessment, emotional health, physical health, healthy behavior, work environment, and basic access (Gallup-Healthways, 2013).

As part of the more general concept of wellness, the definition of physical fitness, according to the Medical News Today, is as follows: "One's ability to execute daily activities with optimal performance, endurance, and strength with the management of disease, fatigue, and stress and reduced sedentary behaviour" (Tipane & Newman, 2021).

As can be seen from the above definition, the concept of fitness is not just something that is limited to a competitive environment, such as competitive

DOI: 10.4324/9781003475699-2

or professional sports practice. In other words, it is not just for athletes. On the contrary, fitness impacts all individuals, some more and some less, and is a fundamental part of their lives (Andreasson & Johansson, 2014). From the amateur athlete who likes going to the gym or out for a run to the office worker who spends his or her working days sitting in front of a screen for eight hours, amateur sports practice turns out to be essential. Every single gesture of a person's daily life involves physical exertion, and without proper preparation and developed muscle tone, small daily gestures can turn into torture over time, even leading to chronic problems (Beauchemin et al., 2019). Thus, the fundamental need to move freely and perform every small or large daily action in the best possible way, without negatively affecting our health, is the reason fitness holds or should hold a fundamental place in people's lives.

In addition, given the high stress levels of workers today, who are forced to wake up early and overcome the 12 Labours of Hercules to get to work, including delayed public transportation, interchanges, cancellations, and disruptions of all kinds, perhaps after sleeping little the night before, constant sports practice is essential to manage stress levels that, as medicine teaches, create inflammatory states in our bodies. While a stressed person sees only problems and feels depressed and discouraged, a person with better stress management also has the ability to identify possible solutions (Kirkland, 2014). More generally, while a stressed person tends toward depression, a relaxed person is happier, more optimistic, and can engage better with others, including family, friends, and workplace colleagues. Moreover, as medical research has proven for years now, a person's actual age is not as important as their biological age: that is, the age our bodies appear to be in terms of strength, speed, muscle mobility, and general functioning. Therefore, rather than referring to our ID cards, specialized examinations and tests are a better way to understand the proper functioning of our bodies (Scheerder et al., 2020).

The take-home message is that fitness is not just about the people who decide to make it their job, such as professional athletes, nutritionists, or athletic trainers. On the contrary, fitness is about all of us. The worker who goes to the factory every day and performs physical exertion needs a strong body to perform those actions to the best of his ability without having physical problems that he will carry for the rest of his life. The office worker who sits still all day needs correct posture at his or her desk, as well as a fit body to stay healthy, given the unhealthy work lifestyle. Even the elderly continue to need to exercise regularly to best preserve their health and delay aging as much as possible. This also includes all athletes who are prevented from playing for a relatively long period of time due to injuries; here too, rehabilitation gymnastics plays a key role. So, as should be clear now, fitness is something that concerns everyone because everyone needs it. Whatever our life choices, our paths and preferences in terms of lifestyle, we must never forget our animal nature; to quote Technogym founder and CEO Nerio Alessandri (2014): "We were born to move".

1.2 The economic relevance of fitness

With these preliminary, but necessary, considerations of fitness as a concept, we can begin to understand the pervasiveness of this phenomenon not only in terms of health but also economically. In fact, just as we have been talking about the physical need to move, business comes in to provide for this need (Smith Maguire, 2008). By definition, the primary purpose of doing business is to provide goods or services to satisfy the needs of potential customers, which may potentially improve people's lives. In the arena of fitness, there is a lot of room for improvement and, thus, many possibilities of doing business in this sector, marking a critical moment when the social and economic aspects of growth come into contact and merge. The social aspect is the primary needs of the human beings who necessarily need to be satisfied (demand); the economic aspect is the action of the entrepreneur who sees the possibility of profiting by creating something useful for mankind and endeavors to do so by presenting his value proposition to potential customers in the fitness market (supply). The economic importance of this subject lies precisely in the vastness of the pool of potential customers and the enormity of profits that this market can generate. This is why PricewaterhouseCoopers' Outlook for Fitness 2022 report began with "Reasons for optimism" (Gavrielides et al., 2022).

Such a statement might seem ill-advised, especially in light of the recent COVID-19 pandemic that has shaken the world and claimed victims on a regular basis in some, albeit limited, areas of the globe. However, the situation is more complex than one might believe. While it is true that people did not have the opportunity to go to the gym or anywhere else to practice the sport they love during the pandemic, it is also true that they had to develop alternative methods to try to continue exercising while locked up in their homes. After about two years of "survival mode", their habits changed and the desire to return to fitness was amplified, because awareness of the psychophysical benefits of regular sporting activity increased considerably. This rediscovery of the importance of fitness has not only resulted in increased gym attendance or a newfound desire to practice a certain sport, it has also changed the way people engage with exercise. While there was a total dependence on a specific location before, now everyone has become more "flexible", exercising in places that may have seemed unthinkable in the past. In this case, the impact of digitalization has been a salvation, creating new channels for the dissemination of exercise, increasing people's knowledge and awareness, and creating new "virtual environments" in which to train. This diversification in how and where to exercise has led people to continue spending on various home training equipment rather than buying online courses or subscribing to home exercise programs. The result of such behavior led to good "resilience" in the fitness market compared to many others, throughout the COVID-19 period (Gavrielides et al., 2022).

Data made available by the consulting firm PwC, which compiles a ranking of consumers' main shopping habits globally, shows that spending on Health and Wellness ranks fifth. Ahead of it are only expenses for one's children (in the case of those with families), groceries, holidays, and home improvement. The first two expenses can easily be classified as basic needs, because providing for one's offspring and for oneself by eating are of fundamental importance. Holidays can be explained by the desire to escape from a place where one has been forced to live for too long, whereas home improvement expenses make sense, given the newfound importance of having a comfortable home—no longer only ones habitat at night, but a place where one can live without the feeling of being in prison. Considering the importance of these abovementioned four purchasing habits, it can be argued that fitness is one of the areas where people believe it is most worthwhile to spend their money. From a business point of view, it is necessary to persist where people are most likely to spend in order to maximize the chances of gaining important market shares and making profits.

The same source investigates the habits that respondents say they want to continue practicing after COVID-19. Among these, exercise stands out. It is as if COVID taught people two things: the ease and convenience of buying things online rather than going there physically and the importance of exercising. Additional food for thought is provided by the data that compares people who continue to rely exclusively on the gym with those who continue to train remotely, whether at home, in the office, in the park, or in other public or private places, perhaps following an online class. In this regard, the PwC research highlights two main aspects: the number of people who have continued to train outside or away from home after COVID has remained constant, while the number of enthusiasts closely associated with the "cult of the gym" has decreased compared to pre-COVID levels. The primary takeaway that emerges from this data is that people have opened up to other forms of sports practice that are less tied to the gym as a physical place and can be practiced almost anywhere with the right adaptation. Obviously, this discourse cannot apply to all types of sportsmen and women, since a rack of weights is of fundamental importance to some types of exercise. However, for the majority of the representative sample of people who train, weights are not essential and can easily be replaced with ad-hoc strength training or small weights that are relatively inexpensive and easy to transport. Therefore, having made these considerations, it can be stated that the importance of the gym is no longer what it used to be; it is being replaced or supplemented with other physical or virtual locations.

Many people who have interfaced with applications, websites, or online lessons have been so enthusiastic that they wanted to continue them afterward. The mixing of physical and digital, of gyms and online courses, has been surprising. In fact, these two environments should not necessarily be considered as direct rivals in which one necessarily excludes the other; rather, they can be considered complementary (García-Fernández et al., 2022). This is precisely the interpretation that can be deduced from the behavior of the PwC's interviewees. Those who regularly attend a gym also like to take online classes more than others. The same source shows that, compared to all consumers, regular gym-goers take classes online from home (51% vs. 29%), at the gym (31% vs. 9%), and even outside the home (7% vs. 5%). In addition, the majority of gym-goers compared to sportsmen in general use parallel courses rather than gyms, as a kind of supplement, an improvement, a plus (64% vs. 36%).

In conclusion, the integration of the physical and digital worlds has been indirectly embraced by the increasingly widespread diffusion of smart-working practices worldwide. Once we were faced with the necessity of working from home in order to maintain a minimum of productivity and not burden the national GDP too negatively, smart working had to kick in. So, just as the home had to become the new work location, so too did this allow people to become mentally resilient enough to welcome fitness into their homes.

So far, the reader has been presented with a preliminary analysis of the concept of fitness within the much broader market framework that is wellness. The difference between these two concepts is often represented by a blurred line, as fitness is included within the broader concept of wellness. In mathematical terms, specifically the concept of sets, fitness is a subset of wellness. However, this blurred line dividing them is justified by the enormous influences that one area has on the other. These two concepts were mentioned in "A Worldwide Overview of the Wellness Economy Market: The Technogym and Peloton Case Studies" to illustrate the enormous economic potential of the wellness market. In particular, the profound psychophysical connection between the two and how consumers' purchasing choices were justified not only by a desire to practice sport but also by people's intrinsic need to feel good about themselves were emphasized (Gazzola et al., 2020).

1.3 Economic data across areas

The Global Wellness Institute (GWI) is an international non-profit organization that has been carrying out market research for years in an attempt to accurately determine the wellness market worldwide. Research, however, is not the only contribution they make, as they seek to stimulate and promote specific initiatives to make an ever-growing public aware of what wellness is and how important it is in everyone's lives. Their contribution at the research level takes the form of various documents. In this case, the most "generalist" document, so to speak, has been examined, which groups its analysis of both a particular nature, by individual country or geographic area, and a general nature, providing an overview of the wellness market at a global level.

The source provides an overview of the global wellness market, quantifying it at $4.4 trillion in 2020 (Global Wellness Institute, 2020). We are, therefore, talking about a gigantic industry (Becker et al., 2021), of which it would be worthwhile to pay particular attention to the fitness market, which alone was worth an impressive $738 billion in 2020. As claimed before, however, it would be wrong to reason that one market had no direct relationship with the others, because the dividing line between one and the other is blurred, and consumers are often faced with a multi-service or multi-product that tries to fit into several similar markets in order to find its own profitable niche.

The breakdown by geographic area shows that the highest numbers are recorded in the Asia-Pacific region, which surprisingly exceeds North America and Europe (Steenbergen & Middelkamp, 2014). This is primarily due to the growing spending power of populations in Asia. In fact, this geographic area is experiencing a steady and important year-on-year increase in the number of citizens that we could define as belonging to the same "middle class" that is progressively wearing out in the Western part of the world. In fact, the decreasing number of citizens belonging to the middle class in Europe and North America is also exhausting its spending capacity in this area, which is ultimately the determinant of these numbers. Now, however, one thing must be made clear: these are aggregate values that do not reflect expenditure per individual. As will be seen below, although the primacy of overall spending belongs to the Asia-Pacific region, the ranking of spending on an individual basis is different. In this case, the factor to be considered is the total number of the population, and Asia is the most populous area in the world, which is the determining factor in this ranking. Therefore, although there is very positive receptivity in both Europe and North America, their spending capacity and, importantly, their total population numbers in comparison with Asia limit the overall market size. On the contrary, high receptivity in Asia combined with their increasing spending capacity and population size are driving their world leadership in aggregate terms. One can also note the increase from 2017 to 2019 in the total market value, precisely because the focus was already shifting toward this industry in the years before COVID. Then, unfortunately, COVID led to an inevitable fall in value due to the decline in purchases caused by quarantine. However, receptivity has increased globally, so one can easily expect strong growth numbers in the years to come. It can be argued that COVID was just a "bump in the road" that will paradoxically lead to an even greater increase in the years to come. Although the value in 2020 did not reach the market value it had recorded in 2019 in any region, this is only a temporary phenomenon; the industry is set to increase its value. If, however, we talk about expenditure at the individual level, as already mentioned, the ranking changes. In fact, in this second ranking, not only North America and Europe come before Asia in terms of expenditure, but also, more surprisingly, Latin America and the Caribbean occupy the third step of the podium.

This is because the average individual income, combined with the strong demand for wellness-related products/services, enables an individual to spend much more than in Asia. In fact, while there are no huge differences between the third and fourth places in the ranking, Europe and North America record much higher levels than those below them.

Another indicator provided by the same Report (GWI, 2020) compares the value of the economy of well-being in relation to GDP. Even in this second case, the ranking does not change. What does change, however, is that the percentages are much closer between one area and another, and the differences in these terms no longer seem as enormous as before (with the exception of the Middle East—N. Africa). It can, therefore, be stated that, given a certain level of economic prosperity, the highest level of development of the wellness economy is currently taking place in North America and Europe. Although these two areas are not the only ones where there is a high level of accommodation and demand, they certainly represent the most important markets because they are also the most developed. This translates into a diversity of supply to the benefit of the consumer, as well as a competitive business environment of continuous innovation. Thus, a whole series of synergies have been activated at the socio-economic level that make these the most advanced markets at the moment.

1.4 How to understand the "fitness-tech" startup world

The promising numbers of a market growing globally have attracted the attention of a long series of entrepreneurs. Unlike in the past, when it was thought that doing business in this sector meant getting involved in an environment relatively unwilling to innovate compared to other sectors, today we can say that this paradigm has changed. In fact, the vocation of new emerging entrepreneurs in the sector is much more oriented to technology and innovation than in the past. As a result, the companies that are trying to attract the attention of consumers have a different footprint. We must also consider the propensity of the current financial market to invest huge capital in those businesses deemed to have high technological value. Certainly, the BigTech industry drives this trend of investment, with companies such as NVIDIA, Microsoft, and Apple reaching new peak points at the level of market capitalization; however, as the fitness world is increasingly linked to digitalization, it is also receiving increasing attention from global financial markets. This has led to the birth of the so-called "fitness-tech startups", which are companies designed to grow quickly and scale by exploiting digitalization as a fundamental lever to get to the widest basin of users in the shortest time possible. The corporate dynamics that follow a successful business in this sector do not differ from the stories in other similar sectors. In fact, while we can expect the growth and affirmation of new names within the global market, with new companies listed on the stock exchange, a growing number of M&A transactions are being made by larger players against new emerging business realities to consolidate their market leadership. The rationale behind these young entrepreneurial realities is the ambition to bring innovation in this area and to profit by offering a better service than in the past. Thus, the focus shifts from the fitness sector in the strict sense to the wider sector of wellness, from physical exercise to the general well-being of the person. In doing so, the offer diversifies, expands, and enriches, which can lead to both increases in corporate earnings and improved customer satisfaction.

Moreover, it is believed that this market is of enormous value not only economically but also and above all socially. A person in a good state of health and mentally serene is a happier person by definition. If, before COVID, the need for sport rather than stress management was considered an important issue by the public, in our current "post-Covid" reality, it is no longer important but essential. This rediscovery of the essentiality of regular exercise and a focus on people's mental health has led to the boom of a whole industry that was previously growing at a fast pace but is now skyrocketing. These societal changes have led entrepreneurs to strive to improve the range of products and/or services offered to consumers. This is a classic market dynamic in which social upheaval has led, first, individual, and then, aggregate demand to increase; consequently, the supply side is trying to adapt in order to seize the new opportunities offered by the market and profit from them. This socio-economic connection represents the importance of this research. Analyzing the dynamics occurring within the global fitness market and the related changes can be very significant and can also highlight a market that deserves extreme attention and priority. This is not just a market driven by temporary fashions or by superficial needs. On the contrary, it is about all those dynamics of an economic nature that occur to satisfy people's most important need: to feel good.

The second concept has to do with technology. Technology plays an essential role in the creation and delivery of one's value proposition to the end customer. A startup that wishes to offer a product and/or service in the fitness or wellness sphere more generally cannot do so without a good technological base. By this, we mean that all those activities aimed at digitizing at least part of their value creation and delivery processes to the end user must necessarily be put in place. An example of this would be gyms investing funds in the creation of dedicated apps to provide online training programs so that their consumer base can work out alternately in the gym and from the comfort of home. Another example might be the same gym that, while not having a dedicated training app, decides to receive electronic payments easily and quickly, perhaps equipped with an efficient electronic invoicing system, or is able to quickly communicate information to its customers about offers or planned changes. A final example can be represented at the communication level by the online presence of content created by the sports center itself in order to better publicize the value of its brand. In order to implement the online presence of these players, expertise is needed in the creation of information technology (IT) systems and infrastructures capable of digitizing content, storing it, managing it, and sending it to all those to whom it may refer. Without adequate technology underpinning a company's digitization, the catchment area is considerably reduced, communication is targeted to a very limited audience, the element of novelty is lost, and the business, therefore, fails.

Lastly, the term startup was not used at random, as the focus of this research was not on the companies that currently represent the biggest market players, the biggest names, and the most famous brands but, rather, the small- to medium-sized emerging companies that are changing the very face of this market, thanks to the innovations they are introducing. Therefore, they deserve special attention.

References

Alessandri, N. (2014). *Nati per muoverci*. Milan: Baldini & Castoldi.

Andreasson, J., & Johansson, T. (2014). The fitness revolution: Historical transformations in the global gym and fitness culture. *Sport Science Review, 23*(3–4), 91–112.

Ardell, D. B. (1982). *Fourteen days to a wellness lifestyle*. Mill Valley, CA: Whatever.

Beauchemin, J. D., Gabana, N., Ketelsen, K., & McGrath, C. (2019). Multidimensional wellness promotion in the health and fitness industry. *International Journal of Health Promotion and Education, 57*(3), 148–160.

Becker, S., Berg, A., Kohli, S., & Thiel, A. (2021). Sporting goods 2021: The next normal for an industry in flux. McKinsey & Company.

BerkeleyWellness.com (2013). What is 'Wellness'? Available at the following link: www.berkeleywellness.com/about-us.

Dunn, H. L. (1961). *High level wellness: A collection of twenty-nine short talks on different aspects of the theme "high-level wellness for man and society"*. Arlington, VA: R. W. Beatty.

Gallup-Healthways (2013). 2012 state of well-being: Community, state and congressional district well-being reports. Available at the following link: https://wellbeingindex.sharecare.com/?utm_source=link_newsv9&utm_campaign=item_159581&utm_medium=copy

García-Fernández, J., Valcarce-Torrente, M., Mohammadi, S., & Gálvez-Ruiz, P. (Eds.). (2022). *The Digital Transformation of the Fitness Sector: A Global Perspective*. Emerald Publishing Limited Leeds.

Gavrielides, E., Trunkfield, D., & Scott, E. (2022). *Outlook for fitness 2022*. PricewaterhouseCoopers LLP UK.

Gazzola, P., Pavione, E., Grechi, D., & Ferrazzano, F. (2020). A worldwide overview of the wellness economy market: The technogym and Peloton case studies. *European Scientific Journal, 16*(10), 5–24.

Global Wellness Institute (2020). *Country rankings* 2020. Available at the following link: https://globalwellnessinstitute.org/industry-research/2022-global-wellness-economy-country-rankings/

Kirkland, A. (2014). What is wellness now? *Journal of Health Politics, Policy and Law*, *39*(5), 957–970.

Maguire, J. S. (2008). *Fit for consumption: Sociology and the business of fitness*. London: Routledge.

O'Donnell, M. P. (2009). Definition of health promotion 2.0: Embracing passion, enhancing motivation, recognizing dynamic balance, and creating opportunities. *American Journal of Health Promotion*, *24*(1), iv-iv.

Scheerder, J., Vehmas, H., & Helsen, K. (2020). The global health and fitness industry at a glance: Fast, fit, flexible, functional, funny, fashionable and fanatic. In Scheerder, J., Vehmas, H., & Helsen, K. (Eds.), *The rise and size of the fitness industry in Europe*. Cham: Palgrave Macmillan, pp 1–32.

Steenbergen, J., & Middelkamp, J. (2014). History, conceptual understanding and perspectives on fitness in Europe. In Collins, C., Buttler, S., & Daalder, N. (Eds.), *The future of health & fitness: A plan for getting Europe active by 2025* (pp. 96–104). Nijmegen: BlackBox Publishers.

Tipane, J., & Newman, T. (2021). What does being physically fit mean? *Medical News Today*. Available at the following link: https://www.medicalnewstoday.com/articles/7181

2 The fitness consumers between wellness, nutrition, and sleep

2.1 Introduction

The changes in habits that have occurred in the last three years have allowed experts to draw a clear picture of what is happening and how the fitness market will most likely evolve in the coming years (Zhang & Trace, 2021; Mosey et al., 2023). An important contribution in this regard is provided by the well-known consultancy firm, McKinsey, which published a report on the health of the global fitness market in 2021 (McKinsey, 2021a), providing interesting insights into its evolution, highlighting the most important trends, and offering a view on how it is evolving. The report's view is extremely optimistic. The pandemic has taught us all how important it can be to look after our physical and mental health and how worthwhile it is to spend our money on taking care of ourselves. This is why it is expected that as people's purchases related to fitness, and wellness more generally, will increase, their spending capacity increases. In particular, the report highlights how a person's well-being is understood as the summary of six closely interrelated dimensions: better health, better fitness, better nutrition, better appearance, better sleep, and better mindfulness.

Firms in all six of these categories are set to see an increase in revenue due to people's changing mindsets, ranging from nutrition and cosmetics to sleep care and meditation practices. But when it comes to fitness in particular, many people were affected by the abrupt change in their daily routine brought about by COVID and continue to struggle to return to their pre-pandemic levels of physical activity. Due to the overlap of these realities, it is speculated that there will soon be a kind of rebound effect in which the number of people exercising will increase exponentially to reach even higher levels than before. This translates in economic terms into a boom in demand that could take place soon, so any investment in this sense is explained by the real opportunity to make money by leveraging this common sentiment. While it is true that the numbers speak for themselves and leave little room for interpretation, this same research shows that out of approximately 7,500 consumers surveyed in six different countries, 79% of them consider wellness to be important, while 42% consider it to be fundamental. What is impressive, therefore, is

DOI: 10.4324/9781003475699-3

not the current numbers of this market, which according to McKinsey amount to $1.5 trillion, with an estimated growth of between 5% and 10% on an annual basis, but the effect that the boom in "new" and/or "found" sportspeople may have on the market in the years to come. Another interesting fact is that although the largest expenditure so far is on wellness-related products, the number of services purchased by consumers is increasing and is expected to balance or even exceed the product component. So, in the coming years, we should expect a service-based market rather than a product-based market. In practical terms, this means that the number of machines used, from dumbbells to barbells, may be replaced by the number of active gym subscriptions and/or online services for coaching, training, nutrition, meditation, etc.

Here is a brief review of the top five emerging trends:

1 **Natural products**: Consumers are inclined to buy various kinds of products, such as cosmetics, skin treatments, supplements and multivitamins, ready-made meals, and sleep enhancers, as long as they are made from quality raw materials. The focus on food is not only on choosing healthy meals instead of junk food, but also on choosing quality ingredients that are rich in nutrients.
2 **Customization**: More and more users are demanding a product/service that is "tailor-made" for them, which means somehow distinguishing them from what is standard. If it is true that the customer experience is a fundamental sales driver, customization is certainly the first step toward that dimension.
3 **Digitization**: Given the advent of e-commerce as a new alternative to the physical shop, products must also be able to connect to a network and have a minimum of integrated AI, while services must be able to provide access to virtual spaces in which to meet with other enthusiasts and share an experience together.
4 **Influencers**: Just as advertising campaigns gained fame after World War II, using television as the greatest means of mass audience communication and dissemination, and stars were admired on a TV or cinema screen, the advent and widespread diffusion of technology in every household has resulted in entertainment stars known as influencers on platforms such as YouTube, Instagram, LinkedIn, X, and Twitch. Our mobile phones, PCs, and tablets have become the new television, while influencers are the new stars. The names of the variables change, but the equation remains the same.
5 **Blurred product categories**: It is wrong to think of a company as producing a certain product without any connection to other related products. Furthermore, it is wrong to think of an app as just offering a service. As the market grows globally, the receptivity expressed by consumers is being met by an increasing number of entrepreneurs, content creators, and web marketers who want to try to make money out of it. Therefore, what used

to be a "mild-red ocean", characterized by normal levels of competition, is now turning into a real bloodbath, with an increasing number of companies entering the market and competing with each other to ride the wave of consumer frenzy, but only a few of them will prosper, while many will be out of the market soon. Therefore, big companies like Lululemon buy promising startups like Mirror in order to meet market changes and remain competitive. At the same time, promising startups sell part or all of their shares in order to get that injection of funds that is essential to grow and succeed in an increasingly crowded and highly competitive market.

2.2 The fitness consumers

After discussing consumers' expressed demands regarding their fitness needs, it is appropriate to profile the various types of consumers by distinguishing them according to identifiable characteristics (Grénman et al., 2019). Recognized as an authoritative source in this industry, McKinsey collected and analyzed data on the different types of consumers. As already mentioned, consumer habits have changed since the pre-COVID era, making it necessary to carry out a new analysis to capture the essential differences in terms of marketing and customer targeting to try both to activate new customers and to retain existing ones. A first point of reflection is provided by the expansion of useful devices and gadgets that support feeling and being better. In fact, the proliferation of increasingly "tech-oriented" startups in the healthcare sector has prompted a growing number of consumers to buy increasingly "smart" devices in order to monitor their most important body parameters, such as blood pressure, heart beat, and stress levels, 24 hours a day. Many everyday devices, first and foremost watches, have become increasingly smart and capable of detecting many body parameters, providing a considerable medical record and offering the possibility of having a much more accurate medical history than in the past. If worn regularly, these instruments track users' parameters over time with a good level of approximation, so after months or even years of monitoring, users and their doctors can discuss problems that arise with a great deal of data already in hand. This is a huge advantage for doctors, who no longer have to start from a few pieces of information provided by the patient or from previous sporadic analyses. The benefit for the patient is equally evident, as one has the possibility of being treated much more effectively than in the past, precisely because of the amount of data provided. This is a fundamental driver that continues to enable young health-tech startups to grow in terms of turnover and funding, receiving trust from both consumers and financiers. However, it also opens the door to the processing of personal data, including questions of how the data is managed, who sees it, and how it is protected against hacker attacks and data breaches. Having such sensitive data in your hands is a big profit opportunity, but also a big responsibility.

The fitness and wellness spheres in general emerged simultaneously. Since athletic performance and wellness go hand in hand with physical and mental health, the synergies between fitness and healthcare are many. A change in consumer mindsets in healthcare also positively influences sports enthusiasts. Conversely, sportspeople are increasingly interested in health in general and are willing to buy devices and clothes and use apps to monitor their health (Trace et al., 2017; Rahaman et al., 2023). Therefore, these two huge markets have so many points in common that it is sometimes difficult to understand where one ends and the other begins, like blurred lines. According to data provided by McKinsey, the market for health and wellness-related services and devices is growing by 5%–10% year-on-year depending on the region. Another interesting figure is the capital raised by fitness-tech apps, which reached $2 billion from investors in 2020, according to McKinsey, achieving a new record. This is because in the current system, every business seems to need an app for multiple purposes, one of which is to activate a new customer by offering special discounts to attract and possibly profile new customers (Chan et al., 2022). However, the primary purpose of an app has always been to offer a service in the form of multimedia content that can be enjoyed by the customer live or on-demand. In particular, with developers' implementation of increasingly innovative solutions and the digitization of many services, many opportunities have arisen to create online content for profit. Hence, many fitness classes have become digitized by creating virtual classes offering courses that connect people from all over the world. With the advent of new virtual worlds, everything that exists in the physical world is also being reproduced in the digital world (just think of the Metaverse introduced by the former Facebook, now Meta). Hence, a yoga or spinning class, traditionally held on site at the gym in the predominantly evening hours to meet participants' work demands, now becomes an online class held over several time slots with the possibility of resuming it at a later date, thanks to the on-demand function. In short, the digital product that previously could be viewed on a delayed basis, like a football match, for example, can now be an online fitness class in which you are the protagonist. Here, one can grasp the paradoxical shift: COVID-19, which started out as a pandemic that led to the domestic isolation of billions of people around the world, creating negative feelings such as depression due to a sense of loneliness, has become the opposite; thanks to digitization, it has become worldwide inclusion.

Digitization identified the problem of the pandemic and tried to find solutions to get the most out of that unpleasant situation, implementing software and products that make us feel like we are in the company of other people while being home alone. It implemented solutions to break down barriers and connect us all together in one big worldwide network. Of course, the benefits are as much social as they are economic. Identification of the problem, creation, testing, and implementation of the solution are fundamental steps in the introduction of any innovative product that aims both to satisfy a need and to profit from it. Based on these considerations, the average fitness consumer has partially changed their purchasing habits, broadening their outlook to adapt to the pandemic while also trying to continue taking care of themselves (Maguire, 2002). This evolution was inevitable, as it was the only way out of the rampant depression that was just around the corner. People were trying to open "digital windows on the world" at a time when governments were forcing people to lock themselves inside their doors. The portrait of the various types of consumers is, therefore, different from what it was in the past. Both pre- and post-COVID-19 pandemic are in customers' minds.

A study conducted by McKinsey (2021b) highlights the following four different categories of consumers:

1 **Passive participant (55%):** This first category describes all those people who do not center fitness in their daily routine. It is not something fundamental for them, but an enjoyable activity to do occasionally, often in response to an external event. The three activation levers for this typology are accessibility, relations, and emotional management. Over time, some of them may develop a greater attraction to fitness, increasing their frequency of training and their awareness; in this way, they may become one of the other three types.
2 **Traditionalist (11%):** This second category describes people who engage in physical activity with a minimum of regularity. They may be runners, gym-goers, or participants in various organized group classes. Often, these people are the most reluctant to adopt new technologies, purchase innovative products, or experiment with training methods other than the more traditional ones. In fact, the best way to win them over is not by introducing new innovative products but by improving existing and widely known ones.
3 **Wellness enthusiast (23%):** This third type describes those who aim to achieve general, all-round personal well-being. They aim to establish a deep mind-body connection and maintain this state of balance. This balance comes through performance in training and attention to nutrition. Fitness is a fundamental and indispensable part of their weekly routine. They love innovations of existing product models with which they are already familiar. At the same time, they might be a little skeptical about products perceived as too innovative.
4 **Researcher-experimenter (10%):** This last type describes those who are always looking for the latest in fitness. They can be considered as the early adopters par excellence in the sector. The only way to try to retain them is to introduce new and innovative products, as their fitness experience needs new things to be excited about all the time. Given this strong push for change, these users are typically the least loyal compared to the other three categories.

2.3 From global-oriented to country-specific

The Global Wellness Institute, which added more than one level of detail in its research by dividing the general dimensions of the wellness market into macro-areas or macro-categories, comes to our aid here. The purpose of this section consists in providing a top-down approach to the topic by starting from the first area of the world to be analyzed: Asia-Pacific.

The global size of the wellness market in Asia-Pacific is valued around USD 1.5 trillion. The Global Wellness Institute divides the profile of the economy of wellness into the following sub-categories, each of which has its own coefficient that contributes to the total market value (Global Wellness Institute, 2022): health eating, nutrition and weight loss, personal care and beauty, physical activity, wellness tourism, public health and prevention, wellness real estate, mental wellness, spas, workplace wellness, thermal/mineral springs, and traditional and complementary medicine. In Asia, the component of most interest to us—i.e., the share of value referring to physical activity—is the fourth most impactful factor in the calculation of the total market value. This means that of the 11 factors considered when calculating the overall Asian market size, the market involving physical activity represents the fourth most impactful component. It does not contribute as much as markets in health food, medicine and specific treatments, and personal care and organic cosmetics, but it plays a more significant role than other sub-categories, such as disease prevention, tourism, and real estate (Little, 2012, 2015; Hamed, 2015). If the Asia-Pacific region is broken down by country based on the contribution per turnover, China currently holds the top position in Asia, with a market size twice that of Japan, which, in turn, is three times the size of the South Korean market. Surprisingly, the latter ranks ahead of Australia, which is very similar in terms of turnover to India, a country currently experiencing a period of growth, thanks to the many new startups that are flourishing. It would not be unreasonable to speculate in the upcoming years that India could rank in the Top-3 Asian countries per market contribution to the overall geographic area.

This data can be usefully compared to the European market. As previously pointed out, the total market value of the Europe region in 2020 was approximately $1.15 trillion. In this case, however, physical activity constitutes the third largest component of the entire industry, behind only personal care and beauty and healthy nutrition. The medicine group in this case plays a relatively marginal role, slipping from third to sixth place in the ranking of the most significant industries. The explanation for this decline is the different understanding of medicine between the East and the West. The Western world tends to see medicine as a purely scientific phenomenon, representing a mere treatment of the patient through drugs or a specific therapy; in short, medicine is viewed as being related to a temporary state of illness that can be resolved, thanks to scientific progress. In the East, however, there is a more holistic view of medicine in which it is not only the cure for ailments of the body, but also the key to a person's general well-being. Myth, folk beliefs, and religious and meditative practices meet with the purely scientific medical sphere and find a compromise, or at least coexist peacefully in the same territory. This leads not only to an "East – West" split in sociocultural perspectives about medicine, but also to a different level of consumer predisposition to spend money to obtain benefits from this field. From this point of view, Asia is much more careful, and the delta value between the same markets in two different continents is evident. As far as individual countries are concerned, Germany, followed by the UK and France, stands on the podium with values above $100 billion each. However, the lowest Top-10 value, recorded by Austria ($32 billion), is still higher than Malaysia ($24 billion), which holds the same position in the Asian ranking. This denotes a higher average level in Europe than in Asia.

North America is the second largest geographic area in terms of market size worldwide, right after Asia-Pacific, totaling approximatively $1.3 trillion. This market is highly developed because American consumers have always been very receptive to products related to physical activity, and they have a cutting-edge entrepreneurial environment in terms of both technology and access to credit, thanks to the financing by various venture capitalists, private equity investors, banks, etc. Sport in this environment is much more performance-oriented than in others, where, for example, the personal well-being aspect may play the dominant role. The culture of redemption, success, spectacle, and glory linked to the world of sporting competition has laid the foundations for a particular consumer focus on all products/services related to sporting activity. This also translates into overall market value, where the fitness market occupies third place, closely following those in front of it and even hinting at a hypothetical overtaking in the years to come. The only two countries contributing to the overall market value of this area are the USA ($1.216 billion) and Canada ($95 billion), with the former having a much higher value than the latter, as one could trivially assume.

As far as Latin America is concerned, the total market figures and the individual countries that make it up change considerably not only in relation to North America, but also in comparison to Europe and Asia. The individual sub-categories that make up the market as a whole are much smaller numerically. In fact, while the market as a whole is about $236 billion, physical activity, which ranks third place, amounts to only $28 billion. Even the most important sub-category, personal care and beauty, totals just $86 billion. Within this context, however, Brazil reigns supreme, outspending all others in every category, as the table below shows. An example of Brazilian entrepreneurship in this area is the worldwide famous fitness company Gympass, co-founded by Cesar Carvalho.

The penultimate area of analysis is the Middle East and North Africa. Here too, like Latin America, the overall market figures are much lower than in the first three areas, which are economically, socially, and politically more advanced. Again, fitness occupies the third position in the ranking; however, the gap is larger compared to the first two sub-categories. Even in this difficult context, where other markets take priority, it is encouraging to see the wellness market find space, albeit very marginal compared to other geographical areas. In terms of individual countries' contributions, Saudi Arabia leads the pack. A few years ago, this country embarked on a process of political openness and technological and economic revolution that has interesting elements and is, for some, a pioneering vision of the future. Certainly, great things should be expected in the future. The state of Israel and the UAE are also in a process of revolution and are the second and third countries in terms of spending in this market. The "light motive" of these three highest ranking countries is the voluntary and gradual approximation to Western living standards. These countries' pursuit of a shift to a socio-political model that approximates Western living standards, without losing attachment to their culture or traditions, can bring mutual benefits in the coming years.

The last area to be analyzed was sub-Saharan Africa, where the overall level of market penetration of fitness business initiatives is low compared to the other areas of the world, at least for now. Although people's economic priorities in this territory are quite different, it is encouraging to see that there is still a desire for growth in the sector. Among the Top-10 countries in this region, South Africa and Nigeria outspend the others by significant margins.

At this point, it is clear that purchasing habits vary considerably according to the economic capacity of individuals and families in different areas of the world. The purpose of this analysis was to focus on the various geographic areas and analyze each country's value at country level, trying to avoid dispersion.

2.4 Nutrition and sleep intersect significantly with fitness

Nutrition and sleep intersect with fitness at both the market and the health science level (Ingram et al., 2020). The axiom is well known and widespread among sportsmen and women: training, nutrition, supplements, and sleep. These four variables inevitably make up everyone's basic athletic preparation, from the professional athlete who earns millions to the amateur who does it for pure enjoyment. Depending on how these variables are balanced within a micro- or meso-cycle of preparation, the results may vary considerably. Putting aside supplementation, which is a component of nutrition, we can focus on the relationship between fitness, healthy nutrition, and sleep quality. Among the major contributors to research in these sub-categories, the Boston Consulting Group (BCG) focuses more on nutrition, showing how it has become increasingly personalized, while McKinsey & Company delves into sleep and the various digital devices that support quality sleep. This critical research is happening at a time when, for the first time in history, everyone is suffering from a lack of average sleep duration, with all the attendant consequences on our psycho-physical health and, consequently, on our family and social relationships.

The key takeaway from their studies is that since the relationships between sleep, nutrition, and fitness are closely related, we should also expect similarities between potential consumers and their purchasing habits. The introduction of a particular innovative product/service that is perceived as appealing by the consumer base results in an interesting phenomenon for the fitness market, as it is part of it. As far as nutrition is concerned, although the idea of producing and marketing foods or meals totally tailored to the dietary needs of each athlete may seem futuristic, research in the business world is already there, so it is a real possibility. A number of startups are developing specific innovative products. For example, the German company MyMuesli has launched a muesli mix that can be fully customized by the customer according to their nutritional deficiencies. Customers can present medical documents to find out what micro- and macro-nutrients they need in their muesli. In parallel, they have also started DNA research to arrive at a customized diet based on each customer's specific needs. Medium-sized and large companies are also realizing the potential here and starting to move in this direction.

The BCG specifically analyzed the relationship between consumers' willingness to pay a "premium price" for a customized product and the delivery costs of a product that is not at all standardized. The propensity of consumers to pay more to benefit from a product/service increases exponentially as the degree of customization of the product/service increases until it reaches a medium level of customization (Boston Consulting Group, 2020). From that point onward, the marginal utility begins to follow a logarithmic curve and then decreases as customization increases until such a high level of customization is reached that the marginal utility is zero, meaning that the consumer would not benefit from paying even $1 more to have a customized product. In contrast, the delivery costs follow an exponential trend from start to finish, from a modest degree of customization to a high degree of customization. In fact, the function rises dramatically in the case of a highly customized product. In more practical terms, a diet plan as a service would be best offered for a type of athlete—for example, a body builder—rather than as individual diets designed differently for each person. Diet plans designed by category—i.e., for bodybuilders, runners, contact sports practitioners, yoga practitioners, cyclists, footballers, etc.—are considerably more profitable than individual diets. This is with a view to increasing competitiveness in the market.

While BCG exclusively studied the market of personalized nutrition, estimated at around $2.5 billion in 2019, with ample room for growth, it is expected that many other related markets in the wellness sphere might follow the same trend. These include, for example, the market for cosmetics and personal care products, software and applications for tracking body parameters, and smart devices and clothes. Ultimately, while it is well known that consumers appreciate a certain degree of customization that contributes to our individual needs, too much customization is counterproductive for the entrepreneur and burns margins.

As previously mentioned, another interesting and related area is the sleep market. It may sound strange at first, but the phenomenon is as relevant as ever, and it affects everyone. We are currently experiencing a sleep loss epidemic never before seen in history. It seems that sleep has become something optional, an obstacle to our daily productivity. We are so busy with a thousand activities that going to bed seems like a waste of time. However, sleep performs an essential function in our organism, and according to much medical research and several TED Talks on the subject, a constant and sustained reduction in the ideal hours of sleep for our biotype leads to a gradual lowering of immune defenses, lack of optimal levels of concentration, low mood, increased susceptibility to depression, and the possibility of a premature death (Perez-Pozuelo et al., 2020). If this sounds catastrophic and worrying, good, because there is cause for concern.

It does not matter whether the cause is too many working hours, work-family balance, or too many hobbies, sleep deprivation has the same consequences. The debate around the problem has become increasingly heated in recent years precisely because the urgency to talk about it has grown. The phenomenon has spread globally and needs to be addressed. The first step to treatment is awareness and the desire to monitor the amount and quality of one's sleep. This framework allows us to understand the parameters of the problem. While medical science strives to find methods and medicines and, more generally, to identify solutions to preserve the people's well-being of citizens, the business sphere seeks to make money by attempting to support medicine in providing solutions. This is why a whole range of young startups, as well as well-established companies, have started to invest in this social problem in order to find a solution.

Another reason to justify their efforts is the focus not only on the B2C side but also on the B2B side. It has been found that a worker suffering from months of sleep deprivation will not only be less productive at work but will also incur higher medical expenses in the long run. Since companies pay the costs of their health and prevention programs, it is in their interest to act as soon as possible to adopt innovative tools that address such problems, hoping that today's investments will save money tomorrow. Another important stakeholder is insurance companies. The biggest risk component of their business is the inability to control and monitor certain behavior related to the various types of insurance policies. Providing customers with tools that constantly monitor certain bodily parameters is like installing a black box in a customer's car when they sign a car insurance policy. That is, it enables a more accurate assessment of the risk and, consequently, a more precise estimate of the price. This can improve efficiency and reduce uncertainty. Moreover, the above-mentioned market players are only some of those in the B2B sphere that might be interested in such equipment and technologies (Sunny et al., 2014). Thus, B2B and B2C are equally promising. An interesting study conducted by McKinsey (McKinsey, 2021c) identifies six potential participants in the sleep-tech ecosystem, all of whom are also potential customers in broader fitness and wellness markets:

- **MedTech**: gain insights into patient activity (e.g., timing sleep and wakefulness) and learn about product use.
- **Payer or insurer**: assess the effectiveness of remote sleep-monitoring interventions by combining patient-activity data (e.g., adherence) with health data.
- **Healthcare provider**: combine structured historical data with nonclinical data to ensure that products offer patients both diagnostics and intervention (e.g., insomnia diagnostics plus cognitive behavioral therapy, or CBT).
- **Pharmacy**: interact with patients to provide sleep products.
- **Pharma company**: use patient-generated sleep data to derive behavioral insights (e.g., relationship between sleep tracking and medical interventions).
- **Health tech**: access relevant targets (e.g., sleep enhancement or patient diagnostics) and establish business models.

References

Boston Consulting Group (2020). *The winning formula in personalized nutrition.* Available at the following link: https://www.bcg.com/publications/2020/winning-formula-in-personalized-nutrition

Chan, G., Huo, Y., Kelly, S., Leung, J., Tisdale, C., & Gullo, M. (2022). The impact of eSports and online video gaming on lifestyle behaviours in youth: A systematic review. *Computers in Human Behavior, 126*, 106974, 1016.

Global Wellness Institute (2022). *Country rankings.* Miami: Global Wellness Institute.

Grénman, M., Hakala, U., & Mueller, B. (2019). Wellness branding: Insights into how American and Finnish consumers use wellness as a means of self-branding. *Journal of Product & Brand Management, 28*(4), 462–474.

Hamed, H. (2015). Wellness tourism: An initiative for comprising wellness tourism vacations within the corporate wellness strategy. *American Journal of Tourism Research, 4*(2), 52–67.

Ingram, J., Maciejewski, G., & Hand, C. J. (2020). Changes in diet, sleep, and physical activity are associated with differences in negative mood during COVID-19 lockdown. *Frontiers in Psychology, 11*, 588604.

Little, J. (2012). Transformational tourism, nature and wellbeing: New perspectives on fitness and the body. *Sociologia Ruralis, 52*(3), 257–271.

Little, J. (2015). Nature, wellbeing and the transformational self. *The Geographical Journal, 181*(2), 121–128.

Maguire, J. S. (2002). Body lessons: Fitness publishing and the cultural production of the fitness consumer. *International Review for the Sociology of Sport, 37*(3–4), 449–464.

McKinsey (2021a). *Feeling good: The future of the $1.5 trillion wellness market*. Available at the following link: https://www.mckinsey.com/industries/consumer-packaged-goods/our-insights/feeling-good-the-future-of-the-1-5-trillion-wellness-market

McKinsey (2021b). *Sweating for the fitness consumer*. Available at the following link: https://www.mckinsey.com/industries/consumer-packaged-goods/our-insights/sweating-for-the-fitness-consumer

McKinsey (2021c). *Sleep on it: Addressing the sleep-loss epidemic through technology*. Available at the following link: https://www.mckinsey.com/industries/life-sciences/our-insights/sleep-on-it-addressing-the-sleep-loss-epidemic-through-technology

Mosey, S., Shipway, R., & Symons, C. (2023). *Entrepreneurship and innovation in sport and leisure*. Routledge, London.

Perez-Pozuelo, I., Zhai, B., Palotti, J., Mall, R., Aupetit, M., Garcia-Gomez, J. M., Taheri, S., Guan, Y., & Fernandez-Luque, L. (2020). The future of sleep health: A data-driven revolution in sleep science and medicine. *NPJ Digital Medicine*, *3*(42), 1–15.

Rahaman, M. A., Taru, R. D., Prajapat, V., & Emran, A. (2023). Determinants of health-conscious consumers' intention to adopt fitness apps. *Innovative Marketing, 19*(3), 1–10.

Sunny, C., Predrag, K., McDonald, D. W., &. Landay, J. A. (2014). Designing for healthy lifestyles: Design considerations for mobile technologies to encourage consumer health and wellness. *Foundations and Trends® in Human–Computer Interaction*, *6*(3–4), 167–315.

Trace, C. B., Cruz, K., Yonemaru, D., & Zhang, Y. (2017). Data ecosystem in self-tracking health and wellness apps. *Proceedings of the Association for Information Science and Technology*, *54*(1), 816–818.

Zhang, Y., & Trace, C. B. (2021). The quality of health and wellness self-tracking data: A consumer perspective. *Journal of the Association for Information Science and Technology*, *73*(6), 879–891.

3 Fundraising and business model

The two traditional drivers

3.1 The financial driver

When it comes to financing, the imperative here is the search for funds by a startup that intends to grow and scale its business (Atherton, 2012; Krishna et al., 2016). Obviously, depending on the type of investor and funding, contracts can differ widely in terms of clauses, duration, rights and obligations, remuneration, and the nature of the investment granted/received (Ener & Dávila, 2023; Giakoumelou et al., 2023). Startups in search of funds tend to rely on three main financial instruments: bank loans, issuing new equity, and selling bonds. However, considering the increasing complexity of financial markets and the multitude of options available to startups seeking funds, the above statement is far too simplistic (Rossi et al., 2020; Momtaz, 2022). In fact, a "democratisation" of funding has been taking place for several years now, with crowdfunding platforms such as Kickstarter allowing everyone to invest in new ideas and participate with very limited capital. In addition, the advent of digitalization has created new avenues for funding such as the famous Initial Coin Offerings (ICOs) used to raise funds for new cryptocurrency ventures (Hashemi et al., 2020). Therefore, it should be specified from the outset that "financing" means the mere act by which a young venture goes in search of funding, and among all the financiers out there, private equity (PE) investors may play a significant role (Breuer & Pinkwart, 2018; Tykvová, 2018).

According to the well-known *Forbes* magazine, there are a couple of noteworthy definitions of PE investors (Baldridge & Benjamin Curry, 2022):

> Private equity (PE) refers to a constellation of investment funds that invest in or acquire private companies that are not listed on a public stock exchange. So-called PE funds may also buy out public companies, take them private, and then restructure them for potential future growth.
>
> Another way to define private equity is as a form of financing where public or private companies accept investments from a PE fund. Typically, private equity invests in mature businesses in more conventional industries in exchange for an equity stake in the company.

DOI: 10.4324/9781003475699-4

These two definitions underline the focus of this section: PE investors. The reason for this focus is twofold. First, as mentioned, there is a multitude of financial players. Second, in the startup environment, it is common to hear of angel investors, incubators, accelerators, venture capitalists (VC), and, finally, PE investors as the main financers depending on a venture's stage of life (Singh & Mungila Hillemane, 2023). Typically, before arriving in the presence of a PE investor, one goes through a rather long series of investors whose purpose is to offer financial resources in exchange for a stake in the company, partial control of the management, sharing of strategic choices, etc. Then, the company is sold to the next investor, profiting from the delta surplus generated. It is precisely this peculiar focus on the company's management that qualifies VC and PE investment activity as purely financial in Europe, whereas it is deemed as managerial-financial in the Anglo-American area. Another peculiarity is that only institutional investors are mentioned here, as this all happens without the venture ever reaching the market.

Of course, it is every private investor's dream to take the ventures they have invested in to an initial public offering (IPO) and monetize from this important operation (Benkraiem et al., 2023). However, the reality is that only a few ever reach this goal. Many do not get there at all, while others choose not to go this route, preferring to continue scaling up their business through private institutional investors exclusively. The reasons for such a strategic move by a venture can be many, but it is worthwhile to understand because the private market is growing. According to popular consulting firm Bain & Company' Global Private Equity Report 2022, explosive growth was recorded in 2021, including exit and deals values. Unfortunately, right at the height of growth, COVID had a negative impact by affecting investors' certainty, lessening their appetite for risk at a time of extreme uncertainty.

The fact that inflation is at 40-year highs is a result of this uncertainty within the market, as well as the influence of various financiers' choices. In addition, the current Russian-Ukrainian conflict is creating upheavals in energy supply, with the price of utilities skyrocketing to triple, quadruple, even quintuple their former costs. This phenomenon is bringing many companies to their knees, compromising their strategic choices and growth. If one then also considers the supply chain disruption that started with COVID and continues to this day, then the macroeconomic scenario is complete. This is why a booming market has suffered from the geo-political factors that have undermined its rise. However, as will be seen in the following pages, rather than a setback, this is simply a delay, a hiccup in the schedule, a temporary jolt, as the mood of hopeful optimism is translating into numbers that tend to be positive and encouraging. In fact, Bain & Company's 2022 study shows that the value and number of investments have increased sharply. The value of the companies that have reached the exit stage has increased, just as the number of these companies has increased.

A similar dynamic applies to fundraising. The same report shows how, after the COVID-related economic setback, quarterly performance trended upward across the board in Q2 2020. While COVID's temporary effects in this area have already been noted, the Bain & Company (2022) Report provides unequivocal proof. In fact, there was a downward parabola from Q1 2019 until Q2 2020 in the case of exits and from Q2 2019 in the case of investments, while fundraising had a positive boost in Q4 2019 and then dropped sharply until precisely Q2 2020. However, since Q3 2020 the trend has been bullish, following a clear increase that peaked in Q2 2021 in all three sectors analyzed in the report. At the macroeconomic level, the decisive factor was the central banks' push to press ahead with monetary policy choices aimed at stimulating investment so that global economic systems would not go into stagnation or deflation. By offering favorable access to credit, they prevented the system from flailing in uncertainty for too long. Considering the globalization of markets and the mutual influences that exist, pursuing common policy at the level of both the ECB and the Fed, as well as other central banks around the world, ensured the resilience of global economies. Of course, there were negative effects that are still being felt today, but without this common monetary policy the situation could have degenerated much more severely.

Moreover, there is evidence of a double trend on the part of PE investors. While the value of investments doubled, the number of buyouts in 2021 was around 4,000 more than the previous five years. Although investing in tech-oriented ventures remains a priority for most investors, the increase in growth equity is evident from the fact that it is still important to diversify one's investment portfolio and recognize the value of certain sub-asset classes such as secondaries, infrastructure, and growth equity, which are experiencing enviable growth. These factors led assets under management (AUM) to double the rate of buyout at an unprecedented rate. Consequently, it is not surprising that AUM and growth equity reached 82% of total buyouts in 2021. Looking more specifically at the area of investments, Bain & Company's (2022) Report shows the deal value at the global level. One can immediately see the peak in value recorded in 2021, with no less than $1.121 billion in total value achieved. This is a record figure compared to the historical data. Not since 2006 had the then-recorded value of $804 billion been reached. The crisis of 2008 also brought this sector to its knees, recording an absolute minimum in the year 2009, with global buyout deal value of $118 billion. From then on, it has experienced a gradual ascent, with a slight downturn due to the crisis of 2012, but a positive trend in the following years until reaching the record value in 2021. If one considers that this value roughly doubles the previous year's value (which amounted to $577 billion), then the "boom" that took place last year can be grasped. The value of the buyout transactions divided by geographical area, although led by North America, highlights the positive growth trend in Asia-Pacific, where the Q4 2021 value is only slightly higher than in Europe, but in the coming years there may be a "two-way race" with North America. Moreover, the report shows two things that are important for the purposes of this book: the first is undoubtedly the primary importance of technology and the weight it has when it comes to buyouts; the second is the healthcare sector, which continues to grow in importance, ranking behind industrials and technology, but sharing a similar share with services, financial services, and consumer products. Here, exits deserve special attention, as the market was overflowing in 2021. It more than doubled what was achieved in 2020 with no less than $957 billion in assets unloaded globally, exceeding the average of the past five years by an impressive 131%, a sign of how strong the "rebound" has been after COVID's acute phase. In this sense, we can say that the relevant central authorities have provided an important boost of confidence and peace of mind that the market is recovering.

Before finishing this section about financial drivers, it would be worthwhile to address a third aspect represented by fundraising. Following the wave of the other two financial phenomena mentioned above, this third phenomenon also experienced a record year. Within private investments, in fact, the total amount raised reached $1.2 trillion in 2021, an increase of 14% over the previous year, registering the highest total value ever recorded. Bain & Company (2022) show how the trend in fundraising levels over the years has been increasing; despite a couple of years of physiological decline (2018, 2020), the positive trend for the rest is evident. What is certain is that the rise from $1.081 billion in 2020 to a staggering $1.228 billion in 2021 is impressive. Once again, the "rebound effect" played a role in the record year. In this case, infrastructure (+30%) and venture (+34%) are the two areas that have benefited most from this generally upward trend.

Finally, it is appropriate to focus on investment regions. Here again, North America shows the highest frequency, with a growth of 33% compared to the average of the previous five years. Western Europe follows with a more modest increase of "only" +11%. Asia, however, continues its positive growth trend with +14%. What is striking, however, are the negative trends recorded by some areas of the world, many of them heavily in the negative. Here, we have Middle East and Africa, with a heavy −58%, Central and South America with an equally heavy −56%, and, finally, a disastrous −80% recorded by Central and Eastern Europe. So, rather than dwelling on the positive numbers that bode well for North America, Europe, and Asia, perhaps it would be more worthwhile to consider what made the other geographic areas collapse. Why there was such a negative impact, and what can be done to start an effective path toward catching up. COVID certainly played a central role in this setback, but these heavily negative numbers also leave room for other considerations regarding the solidity of the ecosystem around which fundraising used to be built.

3.2 The business model driver

The second driver under analysis is the business model. The concept of a business model started to emerge at the end of the 20th century, motivated by the need to describe and analyze new forms of businesses, especially those enabled by the emergence of the Internet and the adoption of e-commerce (Demil & Lecocq, 2010; Schaltegger et al., 2016). In general, the concept refers to describing how different business model components or "building blocks" interact with each other to create a proposition that can generate value for customers and, consequently, for the organization.

A business model can be described as a blueprint, or a strategic framework, that businesses use to create, deliver, and capture value. It serves several core functions, including describing how a company will create and deliver value to its customers, generate revenue and profits, and outline the company's mission, vision, values, target market, and competitive strategy. Business models define the way that a business interacts with its customers, suppliers, and other stakeholders and describe its competitive strategy as implemented through the process of designing the product or service it offers to its target market, pricing it, producing it, differentiating itself from other companies through its value proposition, and integrating its own value chain with those of other companies in the target value network (Rasmussen, 2007).

Given that business models are complex and dynamic systems (Demil & Lecocq, 2010), it is important to have a clear and concise understanding of them in order to be successful. There are plenty of definitions of a business model. Osterwalder and Pigneur, the inventors of the Business Model Canvas tool, offer the following definition of the business model concept:

> a business model is a conceptual tool containing a set of objects, concepts and their relationships with the objective to express the business logic of a specific firm. Therefore, we must consider which concepts and relationships allow a simplified description and representation of what value is provided to customers, how this is done and with which financial consequences.
>
> (Osterwalder et al., 2005)

The researchers interpret the business model as a tool for representing a firm's business logic, providing a definition that focuses on the concepts and relationships used to describe the business model, rather than the specific processes or activities involved. They proposed the following nine building blocks as necessary for illustrating an organization's business model: customer segments, value propositions, channels, customers, relationships, revenue streams, key resources, key activities, key partnerships, and cost structure.

According to Teece (2010), a

> business model describes the design or architecture of the value creation, delivery and capture mechanisms employed. The essence of a business model is that it crystallizes customer needs and ability to pay, defines the manner by which the business enterprise responds to and delivers value to customers, entices customers to pay for value, and converts those payments to profit through the proper design and operation of the various elements of the value chain.

This author provided a more holistic and process-oriented definition, perceiving of the business model as a way to create, deliver, and capture value. This definition also emphasizes the importance of understanding customer needs and knowing how to meet them.

When designing a business model, it is important to consider both stability and flexibility. An effective business model should provide a foundation for the company to build on while also being adaptable to change. According to Cavalcante et al. (2011), a company's business model serves two interrelated purposes: it should provide stability for the development of the company's activities while being flexible enough to allow for changes.

Some researchers have investigated the different perspectives on what constitutes a business model. Within a firm's architecture, a business model is located between the strategic and the operational layers (Osterwalder, 2004; Abdelkafi & Täuscher, 2016). According to Abdelkafi and Makhotin (2013), there are two major approaches to framing business models: activity-based and value-based. The activity-based view of a business model focuses on the activities that a firm performs in order to create, deliver, and capture value, while the value-based view focuses on the value that a firm creates for its customers, suppliers, and other stakeholders.

Despite the different ways that business models are defined, there are four key elements that are common to all business models: *value proposition*, referring to what value the business offers; *value network*, referring to who the business partners with; *value capture*, referring to how the business makes money; and, *value creation and delivery*, referring to how the business creates and delivers value (Roome & Louche, 2016).

The process of how companies develop their business models is complex and dynamic; therefore it is still not well investigated and understood. According to Achtenhagen et al. (2013), three fundamental skills support the development and maintenance of business models: an orientation toward investigating and exploiting business opportunities, an efficient use of resources, and alignment between leadership, culture, and employee commitment.

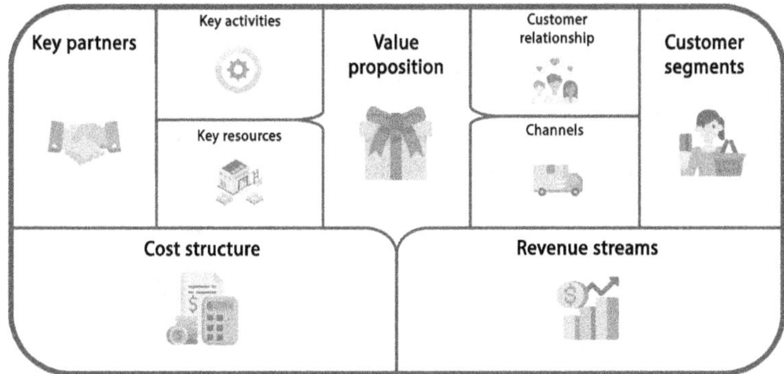

Figure 3.1 Business Model Canvas

Source: Taken from https://www.strategyzer.com/canvas/business-model-canvas with edits

The concept of business model originally focused on organizational value creation, but sustainability researchers have since extended it to include social and ecological values. As the world changes rapidly, business models must adapt to environmental challenges by being dynamic and evolving. According to Winter and Szulanski (2001), "the formula or business model, far from being a quantum of information that is revealed in a flash, is typically a complex set of interdependent routines that is discovered, adjusted, and fine-tuned by 'doing'". In other words, business models are not static documents; rather, they are living systems that must constantly be adapted to changing market conditions and customer needs. "A business model is the direct result of strategy but is not, itself, a strategy" (Casadesus-Masanell & Ricart, 2010).

In order to outline the emerging business models in the world of fitness, included within the broader scope of wellness, this study considers the Canvas model as a starting point. A graphic representation is provided below (Strategyzer, 2022) (Figure 3.1).

To explain briefly, the model consists of the following nine "building blocks":

1 *Customer segments* are the people for whom the company decides to create value.
2 *Value proposition* is the product/service that creates value in the eyes of the consumer.
3 *Channels* are the direct/indirect routes of communication/interaction with the consumer.

4 *Customer relationship* describes the trust and appreciation shown by customers.
5 *Revenue streams* refer to the company's ability to capture value from consumers.
6 *Key resources* emphasize the company's fundamental assets.
7 *Key activities* identify which operations/tasks are essential to achieve the target performance.
8 *Key partnerships* list the names of those partners with which the company interacts.
9 *Cost structure* specifies the expenses to be incurred in order to generate value.

The nine building blocks shown in the diagram above actively interact with each other and continuously exchange information. This communication both internally within the company, or between the company and its partners, and externally with its customers, creates a true value chain capable of analyzing and capturing the characteristics of a specific business. The usefulness of this model is derived from its simplicity and effectiveness in use. It can be a valid analysis tool even with regard to those "hybrid" business models that are particularly difficult to grasp. Rooted in the above-mentioned nine principles, the following analysis applies to the most recurring models.

The first business model analyzed with reference to fitness-tech startups is the membership-based model (Welly, 2021) (Figure 3.2). Of the five analyzed BMs, this can certainly be defined as the most "traditionalist" in the sense that it depicts a model that has existed, been revised, and proven over the

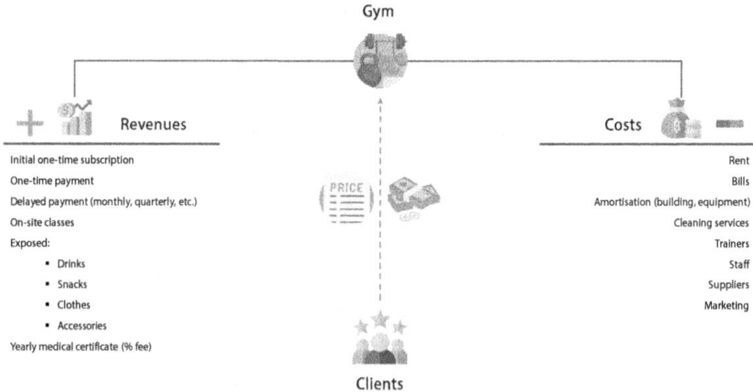

Figure 3.2 Membership-based BM

Source: Own source

years, a veritable "standard" from which many fitness companies want to start their business. In this model, customers gain access to the service, typically a gym or any physical training center, by paying a certain amount of money in exchange for a special subscription that allows them to use the spaces, equipment, and services provided. The expected revenue items include the one-time subscription payment to the sports center, an actual registration fee, as well as the various subscription plans, which constitute the most conspicuous revenue component. There are payment surcharges for participating in physical classes taught by one or more teachers. Once in the sports center, related products on display can also be a source of income. Lastly, medical examinations that are required by law are always chargeable. The costs remain those of any other traditional business; therefore, they are mainly related to space, utilities, and personnel.

In the pre-COVID era, the second BM discussed here had only been adopted by a few companies to diversify their value proposition, but during COVID, it showed its usefulness, i.e., the possibility for customers to train more or less effectively outside the classic sports center or gym (Figure 3.3). Its strength lies precisely in offering both the advantages associated with a traditional model based on attendance at a physical location and the possibility of having specific workouts available for those who are unable to get to the gym but do not want to give up training. It is usually possible to take advantage of such a service within one's traditional subscription, by paying for it separately with a cash supplement, or by taking advantage of a Freemium service, i.e., free basic functionalities to which others are added for a fee. As is often the case, one can find certain items purchasable online as well as there may be advertising banners. There is also the possibility of gaining useful insights by collecting the aggregated data of visitors who use a dedicated app. The disadvantages of this BM are the additional costs associated with creating a digital platform and digital content.

Franchising (Figure 3.4) is another model that was very much in vogue long before COVID. The first major advantage for the franchisee, a figure of particular interest here because he or she is in direct contact with customers, is brand recognition. Leveraging the strength of a brand already built and present in the minds of consumers can protect against the dangers of competition. Moreover, the assistance guaranteed to the franchisee is almost constant, as is the operational support, which also reduces the failure rate compared to other independent businesses. Finally, the customer base already attached to the brand can benefit the franchisee's buying power. However, there are also disadvantages. One of them is the cost of obtaining the license. The support received may also translate into the constraint of having to make certain business choices instead of others, undermining the entrepreneur's independence due to the different bargaining and negotiating power between franchisor

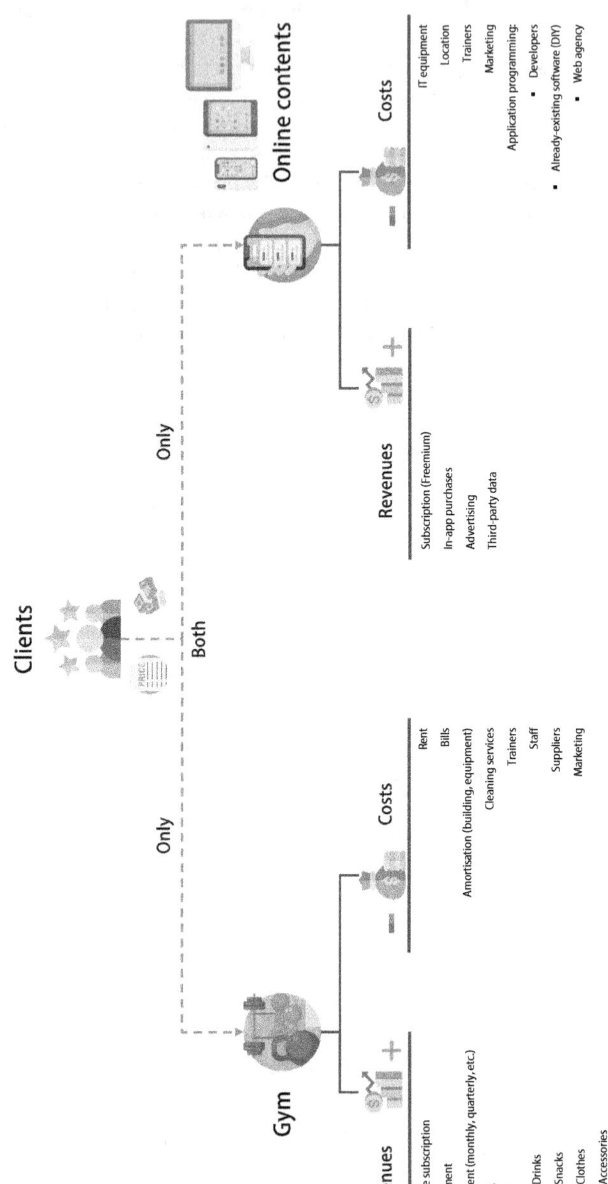

Figure 3.3 Hybrid BM

Source: Own source

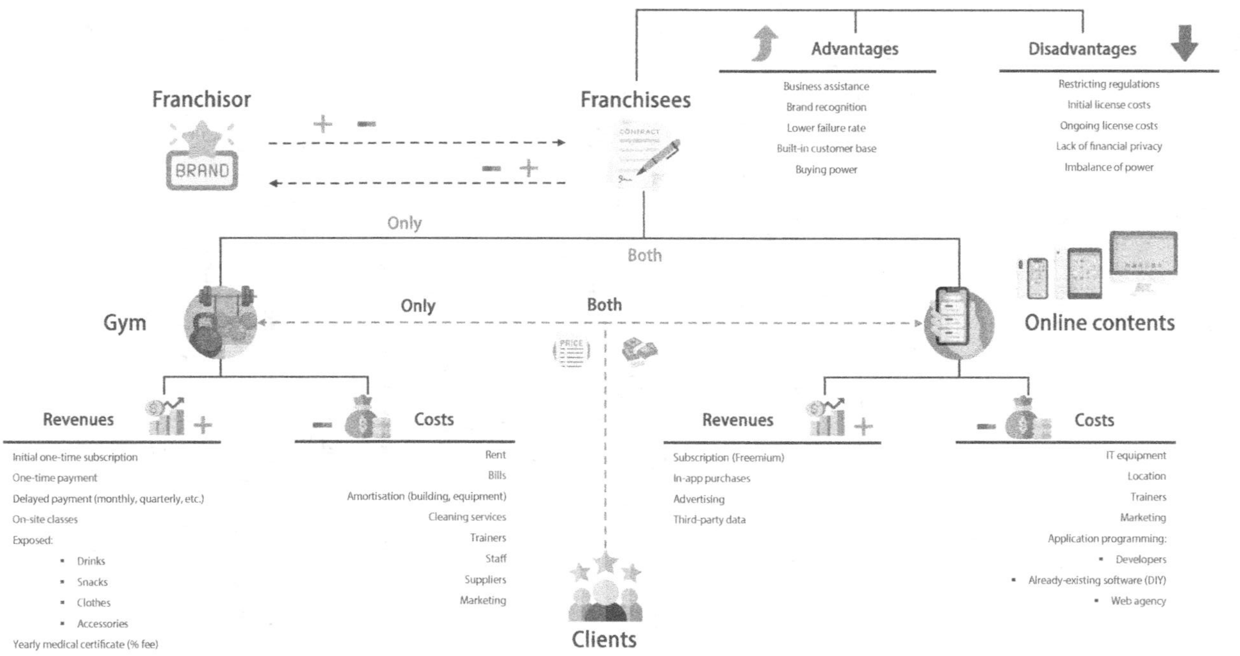

Figure 3.4 Franchising BM

Source: Own source

and franchisee. Finally, accounting privacy is inevitably compromised. At the level of value proposition, the franchisee may be part of a franchise that is exclusively physical in nature (i.e., with fitness centers scattered throughout the territory), or it may be part of an organization that also offers online content. More and more franchises are taking this route given the consequences of COVID.

Another BM that had started to catch on during the first wave of COVID, lasted throughout that period, and is now literally exploding is the digital subscription BM (Figure 3.5). In this case, the model is entirely digitalized. It all stems from the willingness of a trainer, a professional, or even an amateur who is passionate about a certain fitness area to show their training sessions and dispense advice to those who want to follow them. The trainer then becomes a content creator/entrepreneur, and the value proposition is expressed within his or her content. The variety of content creators existing today is vast, and the offer is very diversified. This phenomenon has paralleled the spread of influencers on social media, so this new BM reflects much of what happened previously and continues to persist on the major social networks such as Instagram, Facebook, and TikTok. In fact, these platforms of "relational and social interactions" between people have become veritable marketplaces, while influencers have become celebrities. This social revolution has also influenced the fitness market by taking it from an exclusively physical world to a digital one. This specific BM is the translation of this trend into business language. The cost and the revenues are comparable to those of other digital businesses.

The last BM has reason to exist insofar as it aims to provide a free and tailor-made experience for the customer (Figure 3.6). The principle is obvious: you only pay for what you actually use. From the consumers' point of view, it seems very advantageous because they are fully utilizing something they have paid for, but this BM usually has a higher list price than the same services offered through a more typical contract based on duration or type of service. For the entrepreneur implementing such a strategic move, this also implies an uncertainty in terms of cash flow, as one does not have a recurring and more easily predictable cash flow like other BMs. Given its particular nature, such a BM does not fit well with fitness companies that offer a service that is considered standardized, more traditional, or even aimed at the mass market; rather, it seems to be designed for a niche user base who seeks a more customized experience, perhaps with particular training methods or with training sessions supervised by an expert trainer. Whether it is a subscription to an online service or the use of gym equipment or group or individual training, this BM follows the same principles and aims at the end: extreme flexibility and service customization.

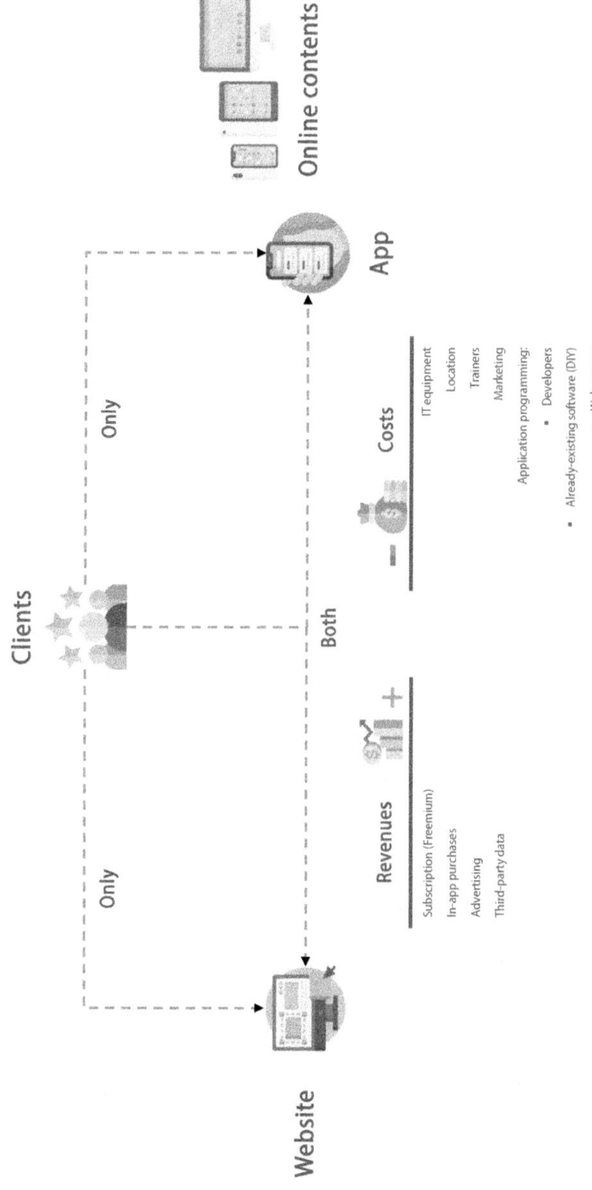

Figure 3.5 Digital subscription BM

Source: Own source

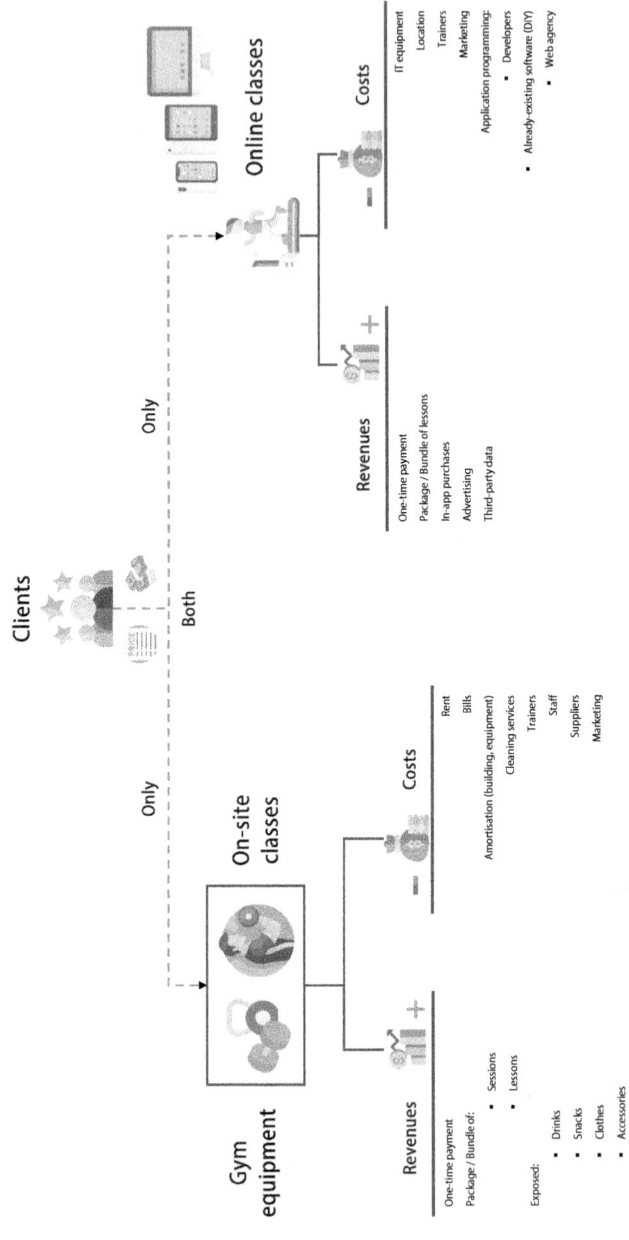

Figure 3.6 Pay-as-you-go BM

Source: Own source

References

Abdelkafi, N., & Makhotin, S. (2013). Graphical representation methods for business model design and innovation—Analysis, comparison & development of an integrated framework. *Presented at 13th Annual Conference of the European Academy of Management (EURAM), Istanbul, Turkey*.

Abdelkafi, N., & Täuscher, K. (2016). Business models for sustainability from a system dynamics perspective. *Organization & Environment*, *29*(1), 74–96.

Achtenhagen, L., Melin, L., & Naldi, L. (2013). Dynamics of business models: Strategizing, critical capabilities and activities for sustained value creation. *Long Range Planning*, *46*, 427–442.

Atherton, A. (2012). Cases of start-up financing: An analysis of new venture capitalisation structures and patterns. *International Journal of Entrepreneurial Behaviour & Research*, *18*(1), 28–47.

Bain & Company, Global Private Equity Report (2022). Available at the following link: https://www.bain.com/insights/the-2022-global-private-equity-report-market-overview-podcast/

Baldridge, R., & Curry, B. (2022). What is private equity? What is a private equity fund? *Forbes Advisor*. Available at the following link: https://www.forbes.com/advisor/investing/private-equity/

Benkraiem, R., Gonçalves, D., & Shuwaikh, F. (2023). The role of corporate venture capitalists in supporting the growth of their backed start-ups. *European Business Review*, *35*(5), 672–693.

Breuer, W., & Pinkwart, A. (2018). Venture capital and private equity finance as key determinants of economic development. *Journal of Business Economics*, *88*, 319–324.

Casadesus-Masanell, R., & Ricart, J. E. (2010). From strategy to business models and onto tactics. *Long Range Planning*, *43*(2), 195–215.

Cavalcante, S., Kesting, P., & Ulhøi, J. (2011). Business model dynamics and innovation: (Re)establishing the missing linkages. *Management Decision*, *49*(8), 1327–1342.

Demil, B., & Lecocq, X. (2010). Business model evolution: In search of dynamic consistency. *Long Range Planning*, *43*(2), 227–246.

Ener, H., & Dávila, A. (2023). What makes search fund entrepreneurship different in Europe? *European Management Journal*, *41*(4), 488–498.

Giakoumelou, A., Salvi, A., Kvasova, O., & Rizomyliotis, I. (2023). The start-up's roadmap to private equity financing: Substituting discounts with a premium in valuation for growth. *International Journal of Entrepreneurial Behavior & Research*. Ahead-of-print. https://doi.org/10.1108/IJEBR-02-2022-0197 https://www.emerald.com/insight/content/doi/10.1108/IJEBR-02-2022-0197/full/html

Hashemi Joo, M., Nishikawa, Y., & Dandapani, K. (2020). ICOs, the next generation of IPOs. *Managerial Finance*, *46*(6), 761–783.

Krishna, A., Agrawal, A., & Choudhary, A. (2016). Predicting the outcome of startups: Less failure, more success. *IEEE 16th International Conference on Data Mining Workshops (ICDMW), Barcelona, Spain* (pp. 798–805).

Momtaz, P. P. (2022). Is Decentralized Finance (DeFi) efficient? Available at the following link: SSRN: https://ssrn.com/abstract=4095397 or http://dx.doi.org/10.2139/ssrn.4095397

Osterwalder, A. (2004). The business model ontology—A proposition in a design science approach (Unpublished doctoral dissertation). Université de Lausanne, Lausanne, Switzerland.

Osterwalder, A., Pigneur, Y., & Tucci, C. (2005). Clarifying business models: Origins, present, and future of the concept. *Communications of the Association for Information Systems*, *16*, 1–25.

Rasmussen, B. (2007). Business models and the theory of the firm. Working Paper. Victoria University of Technology, Melbourne, Australia.

Roome, N., & Louche, C. (2016). Journeying toward business models for sustainability: A conceptual model found inside the black box of organisational transformation. *Organization & Environment*, *29*(1), 11–35.

Rossi, M., Festa, G., Fiano, F., & Giacobbe, R. (2020). To invest or to harvest? Corporate venture capital ambidexterity for exploiting/exploring innovation in technological business. *Business Process Management Journal*, *26*(5), 1157–1181.

Schaltegger, S., Hansen, E. G., & Lüdeke-Freund, F. (2016). Business models for sustainability: Origins, present research, and future avenues. *Organization & Environment*, *29*(1), 3–10.

Singh, S., & Mungila Hillemane, B. S. (2023). Sources of finance for tech startups over its lifecycle: What determines their approach of sources and its success? *International Journal of Emerging Markets*, *18*(8), 1766–1787.

Strategyzer (2022). The business model canvas. Available at the following link: https://www.strategyzer.com/canvas/business-model-canvas

Teece, D. (2010). Business models, business strategy and innovation. *Long Range Planning*, *43*, 172–194.

Tykvová, T. (2018). Venture capital and private equity financing: An overview of recent literature and an agenda for future research. *Journal of Business Economics*, *88*, 325–362.

Welly, J. (2021). What are the different types of gym business models? *Glofox*. Available at the following link: https://www.glofox.com/blog/gym-business-models/

Winter, S. G., & Szulanski, G. (2001). Replication as strategy. *Organization Science*, *12*(6), 730–743.

4 Sustainability

The future of social responsibility

4.1 Introduction

Sustainability is now a fundamental driver of companies' competitiveness in all sectors (Commission of the European Communities, 2002; Gazzola & Colombo, 2014), as it affects reputation, consumer perception, and selection and purchasing. These are the three dimensions of sustainability that represent the pillars of the Triple Bottom Line (Elkington, 2007), which must be addressed to obtain results for a competitive advantage in the medium to long term and are foundational to one's business strategy: Profit, Planet, and People. There is a close relationship between a company's socio-environmental and economic performance (Bennet & James, 1999). The three dimensions of sustainability are not separate or independent but are closely interconnected. Economic sustainability is certainly essential for a company's survival, but it is no longer enough in a modern business model. To compete in the market, it is also essential to be socially and environmentally sustainable.

More than 30 years have passed since the United Nations Environment Program (UNEP) published the Brundtland Report, also known as Our Common Future, in 1987. In that document, for the first time, the concept of sustainable development, more commonly referred to as sustainability, was introduced and explained: "sustainable development is a development that meets the needs of the present without compromising the ability of future generations to meet their own needs". The awareness of the need for a change in the approach to sustainable development is reiterated by point 9 of the UN General Assembly declaration, which reads (United Nations, 2015):

> The world we envision is a world in which every country enjoys lasting economic growth, open to all and sustainable […]. A world in which consumption, production processes and the use of natural resources […] are sustainable. A world where the development and use of technology is climate-sensitive, respectful of biodiversity and resilient. A world in which humanity lives in harmony with nature […]

DOI: 10.4324/9781003475699-5

More recently, the 2030 Agenda established "Sustainable Development Goals" (SDGs) for sustainable development (Lee et al., 2016), with 2030 as the deadline by which nations must have fulfilled standards for achieving the goals (Griggs et al., 2013; Doyle & Stiglitz, 2014).

The concept of sustainability has taken on different meanings over time, eventually overlapping with that of social responsibility. Strictly speaking, it refers primarily to the ecological dimension (Magee et al., 2013). Being ecologically sustainable means making choices that can reduce the environmental impact of one's production activities by containing consumption and creating products whose production methods and/or raw materials will not burden the environment (Meyer & Helfman, 1993). At the same time, this concept of sustainability is also accompanied by respect for the health and conditions of workers and consumers, human rights, and renewed relationships with the local community and all stakeholders (Porter & Kramer, 2002). In a broader sense and strategically key, the concept of sustainability embraces the search for well-being, a better quality of life, and a sense of responsibility toward the community (Magee et al., 2013). In an environmental scenario in which the variable "well-being" is increasingly becoming a measure of wealth that a production system is able to express, attention to sustainability includes behaviors that are not limited to ethical responsibility and compliance with regulations but, instead, have greater strategic significance. From a broader, strategic perspective, addressing sustainability impacts the entire value chain, from the commercial proposal to the relationship with the consumer, up to the management of the end-of-life of a product, within an increasingly extensive and complex network. Empirical evidence shows that the best performing companies in terms of sustainability are those that integrate it into governance processes and rethink business models with the aim of seizing the growth opportunities that a sustainable approach brings with it.

4.2 The importance of sustainability

"Sustainability" is a recurring word in many areas, from environmental science to economic and political maneuvers. Depending on the context in which this single but powerful word is used, the meaning changes considerably. For instance, a politically "sustainable" maneuver is one that can be repeated over the years because it is not excessively burdensome in terms of the resources employed and it is acceptable to most political representatives. Thus, depending on the context, the meaning varies considerably. In the business sphere, Harvard Business School Online provides a brief but precise explanation that emphasizes the environmental and social impact of sustainability, envisioning a sustainable business as one in which processes and the sum of activities do not negatively impact either the surrounding environment or the neighboring community or society at large.

To give a concrete example, a company that pours waste into the sea or does not properly dispose of waste according to environmental regulations is not sustainable. Similarly, an energy extraction company that does not operate with the utmost care in its crude oil extraction and refining processes and causes its employees to develop cancer due to exposure to fine metal dust after years or decades of work is not sustainable. In addition, a company that makes a profit, grows in terms of revenue, and is perfectly healthy but does not invest in projects of a social nature or promote initiatives that benefit the community is not sustainable. These examples show how deep the link of sustainability is with the famous ESG Index, which describes potential Environmental, Social and Governance impacts.

The ESG Index quickly became a fundamental factor for companies in many areas, including media and corporate communication, brand positioning, brand image, process quality certification, employee health, and finance. This last aspect has a purely economic but no less important significance. Indeed, more and more institutional investors, such as investment banks and international hedge funds, are demanding rigorous standards of compliance with ESG criteria. This pushes companies to seek certifications that attest to their compliance with ESG criteria in order to make themselves more attractive in the eyes of potential investors. For example, the prestigious B Corp. certification attests to the quality of business processes that conform to certain standards (Gazzola et al., 2019). As the market increasingly wants to invest in these sustainable companies, more and more companies are being pushed into compliance in order to obtain more capital for growth and expansion. Ultimately, the competitive advantage that can be created in the long run outweighs the investments required for implementation today.

A brilliant report by the Boston Consulting Group (Boston Consulting Group, 2022) even identifies a "global race to sustainability", noting that it is difficult to recall another time in history when companies were so economically motivated to embrace change. The report highlights $35 trillion of assets under management by the capital markets in 2021 with growth to $50 trillion expected by 2025 globally. Meanwhile, sustainability-linked loans and financing surpassed the $1.6 trillion mark in 2021, with triple-digit growth from 2019. Globally, these initiatives are expected to result in $6 trillion in global GDP growth by 2050 and lead to the creation of 3 million new jobs. As a result, the well-known battle against global warming, the 1.5°C of warming considered as a "psychological barrier" or even a "threshold of no return", is viewed with increasing apprehension by corporate stakeholders. However, although the situation may seem rosy in terms of initiatives taken by the various institutional and financial players that are dictating a new vision of doing business, many companies continue to lag behind in this process.

This is partly due to a contractual problem of the management, which is incentivized to achieve short-term business goals and, therefore, does not pay due attention to more radical changes that may only have returns in the long run. Furthermore, not all companies have the resources to make the ecological transition. In fact, most micro and small companies are forced to spend on vital resources to remain competitive in the market and cannot afford to "waste" funds that can generate quick returns to make long-term investments. This is especially, but not only, true for those crowded and very competitive markets, the so-called "red oceans". Therefore, another important cause of delay is the fear of losing competitiveness and going out of business. Furthermore, BCG also found that of the 500 companies analyzed the sustainability policies of only 1 in 5 showed a significant impact on the process of value creation and competitive advantage at market level, while only 1 in 15 were adapting their business model in relation to its sustainability improvement process, thus changing the competitiveness of its industry. Against these considerations, therefore, the emerging picture both depicts the strategic importance of embracing innovation and shows how little has been done in practice so far. Therefore, a first step in embracing this new trend, as emerging as it is important, is to ask the right questions and give honest answers to effectively embark on a path to radically change how business is done, including how business activities and internal processes are organized, with the goal of changing the industry itself.

This last statement may seem overly bold; yet, there are concrete examples of companies that have succeeded exist and serve as an inspiration to all others. For instance, Tesla radically changed consumers' conception of buying an "eco-friendly" car powered by electricity instead of fossil fuels, and in order to remain competitive in the eyes of potential customers, other market players have had to step on the accelerator in terms of innovation in order to bring a car with equivalent characteristics to the market. Thus, the example of Tesla is masterful in understanding how a single startup with a high-tech vocation can aspire not only to carve out its own niche in the market, to make itself appealing in the eyes of consumers, but even to stimulate innovation within its industry of reference and change the industry itself.

To even think of starting such an entrepreneurial journey, it is not enough to have a variable cost model, an agile working methodology, and process flexibility; it requires a marked mental elasticity on the part of the entrepreneur and/or all members of the BoD and top management. Once the psychological foundations have been laid and the ideological conviction that the "new" direction is the right one is in place, then the technical and operational side will follow accordingly. This domino effect must always start from the mindset of the people who work at high levels in the company and have the decision-making power to make important changes, while the technical part is the natural and inevitable consequence of their decisions.

Another good reason to embark on this path of sustainability is the current geo-political conditions, in which a heavy reliance on non-renewable energy sources such as coal, oil, and its derivatives can be a factor of competitive vulnerability. Indeed, if we look at the current energy crisis, where the widespread winds of war in Eastern Europe and Asia are currently represented by the direct military conflict between Ukraine and Russia but indirectly involve a much larger number of states, we can see how most global companies are suffering from the heavy increase in energy prices. Indeed, investing in fossil fuels to power production processes often leads to external factors undermining the stability and proper flow of operations. In addition, these energy sources are, by definition, finite and destined to run out, so relying on them ignores a long-term problem in order to try to survive in the short to medium term. In contrast, a good diversification of energy supply sources, always preferring renewables to fossil fuels, guarantees a long-term return in terms of supply stability, which can prove to be a decisive factor in ensuring a continuous flow of production, hence a higher final output.

If we also consider the series of incentives for the energy transition at both state and supranational levels, a politically hot topic today, the potential benefits increase. Since today's consumers are much more aware of their purchasing choices than the consumers of a few decades ago, being perceived as an "eco-friendly" brand that is environmentally oriented and, therefore, sustainability-conscious can only be an advantage that translates into higher sales volumes. If the companies that are suffering from the energy supply crisis today had effectively embarked on the path of sustainability years ago, they would certainly be totally or at least partially sheltered from the current winds of war and political-economic repercussions that are ensuing today. Therefore, they also would have benefited greatly in terms of costs. The benefits of embarking on an effective sustainability transformation are many, including an improved brand image and a higher market valuation. A positive environmental impact from production processes often correlates with easier adherence to regulatory principles and a lower likelihood of losing market competitiveness in the long run. Moreover, risk management within the overall corporate framework is positively affected, of which the ongoing Russia-Ukraine War is but the most vivid and tangible example of the present moment.

Rather than a linear process, sustainability can be represented as a circular process. Indeed, prior to Russia's invasion of Ukraine, the USA and China trade war over resources that are of primary strategic importance for the IT infrastructure and equipment sector brought the issue of controlling sources of supply to the fore. Again, having control over renewables would have given many companies better health and less exposure. Moreover, it would have benefited them at the level of investment attractiveness, as each investor seeks to diversify their investment portfolio. These companies would have been seen as profitable investments in the long run and safe in the short run, a dual advantage that would have brought them confidence in the form of investments received. Once again, if companies' focus on sustainability was more concrete and economically visible, many entrepreneurs and investors would be calmer today despite current macroeconomic conditions.

Another aspect that deserves to be explored is of a social nature and concerns the so-called "Silver Economy", meaning those markets that serve people who are 50+ years old. Although this industry may seem unimportant at first glance, it is critical from both social and economic perspectives. First, from a social point of view, there is a general aging of the population in those countries considered as rich. Second, from an economic point of view, there is skyrocketing demand coming from this specific population. We firmly believe that communities of people over 50 represent the most important aspect of the ESG index, and, more specifically, of the sustainability side within the fitness and broader wellness industries. That is why we shall go into more detail in the following section.

4.3 A glimpse into the Silver Economy

When we talk about athleticism, it is easy to think of young people who do many sports for recreational purposes, often in the company of friends; when we talk about the elderly, we think much more frequently about the treatment of some disease. These common thoughts, however, are not necessarily true and may become even less so in the decades to come. In fact, the rise in the quality of life in many areas of the world and the rise in the aging population index in those countries considered rich are contributing to the growth of the specific area of the economy that targets people who are 50 and older, the so-called Silver Economy.

This branch of the economy takes its name from the phenomenon that people's hair changes color as they age, first to gray and then, increasingly, to silver. As Iberdrola (2023) explains, an early form of this market already existed in Japan under the name "Silver market". Japan, in fact, has the highest percentage of people 65 or older; therefore, they have had to take action to respond to the needs of this age group before any other country. Of the several definitions that have been provided to explain the Silver Economy, the following is worth quoting: "all types of goods and services for older adults and an aging population, including extending the working life, volunteerism, and active citizenship of older people" (Ruggiero & Fatigati, 2021). The Silver Economy, therefore, includes all goods and services that concern people aged 50 and over. Since the rate of aging is increasing and involves a large mass of people, it follows that there are also many opportunities to do business in this sector.

Before addressing the numbers, it is worth pointing out that we are not talking about a specific sector, but about a market so large that it can embrace different sectors. To give a few examples, the business may involve fitness, nutrition, wellness treatments, tourism, entertainment, mineral and spa products, clothes and wearable devices, smart devices, banking and payments, etc.

The most accurate numerical research available online about this topic was requested by the European Commission and carried out by the Technopolis group in collaboration with Oxford economics. The document provides a comprehensive view of this economic phenomenon, providing an important set of data, analysis, and trends with the aim of highlighting the evolution of this market on the European chessboard. The information addressed here come from this enlightening report (Technopolis group, Oxford economics, 2018).

The first important data is of a demographic nature: in 2015, 39% of the European population was aged 50 or over, corresponding to a number of 199 million individuals. Furthermore, that trend has been increasing in recent years, meaning that if someone took a snapshot of the current situation, the numbers would be even higher. Thus, we can conclude that at least 4 out of every 10 citizens in Europe are 50 or older. This message is pretty significant, and it should immediately express the magnitude of this market. Moreover, in 2015, this specific sector of the economy supported 78 million jobs, with a turnover of more than EUR 4.2 trillion in GDP. Considering that these numbers refer exclusively to the European market, it should be clear how impactful this sector of the economy is. Given the growing trend, the numbers would probably be even more impressive if they made another survey after ten years. Moreover, the value chain that is generated is not only about stakeholders within the EU. On the contrary, it necessarily involves players from other regions of the world. In particular, companies outside the EU benefited from revenues of approximately EUR 780 billion (18.6% of the Silver Economy GDP). In addition, it is estimated that consumption of goods and services related to this specific economic sector within the European market will grow by 5% annually until 2025, reaching a total final value of about EUR 5.7 trillion. Therefore, this sector will become increasingly important as the average age of the European population increases. Following a predictive analysis, it is estimated that the Silver Economy will reach the ambitious target of EUR 6.4 trillion in GDP (31.5% of total European GDP) by 2025, employing 88 million workers (37.8% of total European employment). The above-mentioned values make the Silver Economy in Europe the third largest market in the world, behind only the USA and China. Figure 4.1 represents the main highlights that are worth grasping.

The nature of consumption that drives demand in the European market is worth further consideration. Just as 39% of Europe's over-50s contributed 40.6% of private consumption spending in 2015, with a total value of EUR 3.3 trillion, so it is expected that the increase of this population group to about 43% of the total in 2025 will result in an increase in the group's private spending to 44.3%, reaching a value of about EUR 5 trillion (Technopolis group, Oxford economics, 2018). Naturally, the public sector will also need to revise its budget upward in order to continue to offer its citizens an adequate

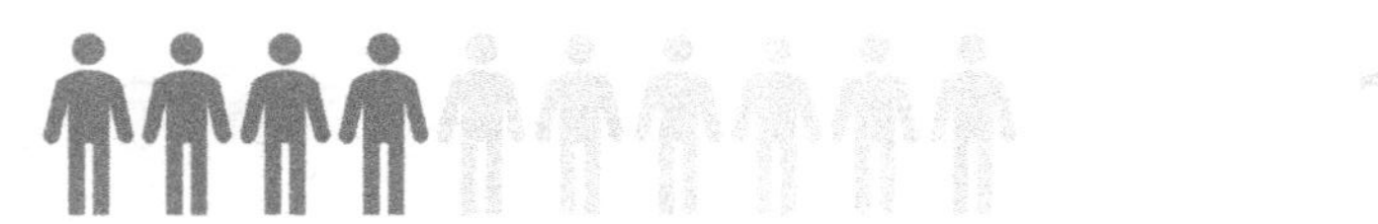

In 2015, almost **4 out of 10** European citizens were aged **50+ years**.

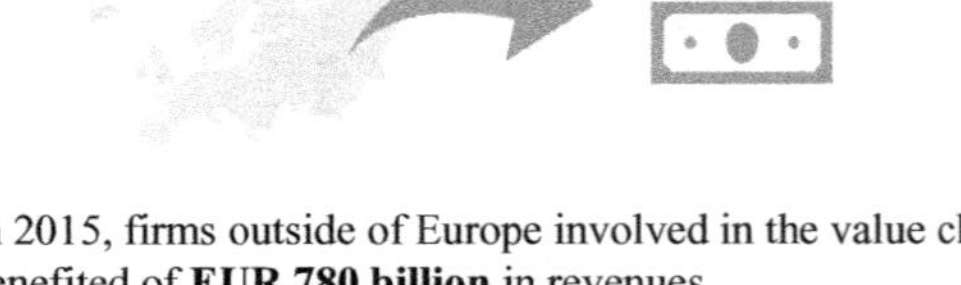

In 2015, firms outside of Europe involved in the value chain benefited of **EUR 780 billion** in revenues.

GDP

2015	2025
EUR 4.2 trillion	**EUR 6.4** trillion

Employment

2015	2025
78 million jobs	**88** million jobs

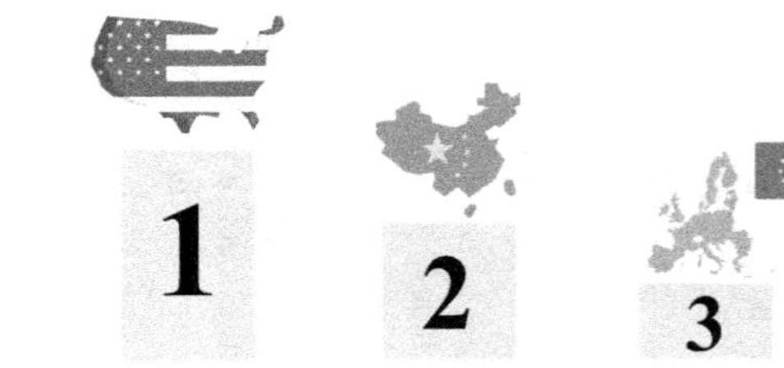

The European Silver economy is **the third** largest market in the world, just behind **USA** and **China**.

Figure 4.1 European Silver Economy highlights

Source: Technopolis group, Oxford economics (2018). The Silver Economy, European Commission, with own edits

level of services, paying particular attention to this population. Thus, public spending in the EU is projected to rise from EUR 421 billion in 2015 (14% of total European public spending) to EUR 635 billion in 2025 (15.5% of the total). Ultimately, the estimated growth rate within the period between 2015 and 2025 is about 50% for both the public and private sectors. In reference to the multitude of items of expenditure that could be identified within the sphere of private citizens, the report mentions the following Top-10 (in order of frequency): health, food and beverages, furniture and home, recreation and culture, accommodation and services, communications, alcohol and tobacco, various goods and services, transport, restaurants, and hotels (Technopolis group, Oxford economics, 2018). To date, therefore, private expenditure on clothing or education for example, is only marginal.

Beyond the European framework, a Brookings's article entitled "The silver economy is coming of age: a look at the growing spending power of seniors" identifies where private spending among middle and high class citizens who are 65 and older is highest (Top-10 in order from greatest to least): the USA, China, Japan, Germany, France, Russia, India, the UK, Italy, and Brazil (Fengler, 2021). The United States dominates private spending, followed by China and Japan. It is not surprising to see Japan in third place for two reasons. First, Japan has the oldest population in the world. As Jonathan Soble (2014) noted in the *Financial Times*, in 1950 about 5% of the Japanese population was aged 65 or over, while that percentage had increased to 25% by 2014, bringing the median age to 44 years, the highest in the world. This implies that a large portion of the population is probably spending money on those things that are most common for people over 65. Second, this change in purchasing habits has prompted the economy to change and pay increasing attention to the needs of the over 65s. From the perspective of an entrepreneur, trying to offer a specific product or service for a pool of potential customers over 65 means finding the most promising consumers in Japan, both because of their increase in number and because of their economic availability, which is higher, on average, than younger members of the Japanese population.

The Brookings article introduced in the previous paragraph also reported that the private spending of middle and high class citizens who are 65 and older in the USA was about USD 2.2 trillion in 2020, and it is estimated to reach USD 3.3 trillion in 2030. The world's number one economy, therefore, continues to drive the world economy in this economic sector as well, as it is also experiencing an aging population. Moreover, the economic resources of the 65+ in the USA grew while the country was climbing the summits of the economy and establishing itself as the undisputed world leader, which has led to a greater accumulation of wealth. Today, however, US citizens are facing a difficult period between lower growth rates and an increasingly heavy debt burden, leading to worsening economic conditions. Given this fact, the USA has a strong interest in seizing the Silver Economy as an opportunity not only to meet the needs of people over 65, but also to create new economic opportunities for younger generations.

The USA is followed by China, which boasted a private spending value of about USD 0.7 trillion in 2020, but by 2030 that could explode and reach the amazing value of about USD 2.2 trillion (Fengler, 2021). This estimated growth is impressive. Indeed, it is the highest growth rate among all the countries compared. This forecast is justified by the strength of the Chinese economy, which has recorded rates of growth unimaginable compared to those declared by the main Western economies in recent years. The Chinese government has undoubtedly been very skilled at guiding and directing the country's incredible economic growth by developing an environment that is conducive to it. This growth has improved the economic conditions and, thus, the living standards of the population. In turn, this improvement has increased domestic demand for goods and services for a population that is currently young but that will continue to age in the coming years, which will lead to changes in their purchasing habits. Having proved to be the most promising emerging economy and able to benefit from trade agreements with Western countries better than all other Asian countries, China has officially established itself on a global level, changing its status to one of a rich, highly industrialized, and first-rate financial country. However, like all rich countries, China is beginning to experience the problems and complexities that are typical of no longer emerging economies. The first of these is a lower birth rate than the aging rate. This leads to an increase in the average age of the population, which leads to changes in buying habits. China, therefore, is experiencing this change from "young country" to "old country", as many other advanced economies have experienced. This development can explain private spending at high levels, but comparable with other countries, which then explodes and records impressively above-average growth rates.

In the third place, Japan recorded a private spending value of about USD 0.7 trillion in 2020, which is expected to reach USD 0.9 trillion by 2030 (Fengler, 2021). Japan is already in the midst of this phenomenon called the Silver Economy, which helps to explain why the growth rate of private spending in 2030 is relatively low and not surprisingly strong. As the country with the original Silver Market, Japan has been a pioneer in the economic management of the over-50 population, which, of course, includes everyone over 65. Today, the country of the Rising Sun continues to innovate and find ingenious solutions to grasp all of the potential opportunities available in the Silver Economy. Indeed, the considerations addressed earlier in this chapter are valuable to better understand Japan's third position on the podium.

While presenting different peculiarities and economic conditions, the countries that follow within the ranking, from Germany in fourth to Brazil in tenth, are united by comparable volume in this specific economic field, representing about an average of USD 0.4 trillion in private spending in 2020, with a timid increase of up to USD 0.6 trillion expected for 2030. India is the only outlier, with a private spending value of about USD 0.1 trillion in 2020 and an amazing anticipated increase to about USD 0.5 trillion in 2030. While it is not comparable to China's projected growth in absolute values, it remains an important upward leap. This is mainly due to India's rapidly growing (and aging) economy. Like China, India is having to manage a large number of citizens, and the share of the population who are aging is beginning to be felt economically. Although the Indian economy does not have the same competitive, industrial, and financial strength as China, its strong growth deserves to be mentioned. As the country's economy continues to grow, it will move closer to the characteristics of a rich country, one of which is that the population over 65 is likely to have an increasing influence over some aspects of the economy.

Rothschild & Co's (2023) interpretation of data from the World Bank provide additional information for understanding the strong links between demographics and economics as they relate to wellness:

> According to the World Bank, average global life expectancy shot up from 65 in the early 1990s to 73 in 2020. The hike in longevity stems from better healthcare, working conditions and nourishment as well as access to clean water. Life expectancy is now 80 years in the EU, 77 in the US, and 76 in Latin America and the Caribbean. By 2030, the number of people aged 60 years and above will grow globally to 1.4 billion, outnumbering the total of children aged under 10 years.

The growing population over 60 worldwide can affect the economic aspect of any country. In this regard, it is useful to understand the most common purchasing habits of these citizens. A study carried out by Rothschild & Co (2023) found the following six items of expenditure to have positive outcomes and forecasts between 2011 and 2025: health care, food, goods and services, leisure, communication, and housing. These, then, are the markets to be targeted for investment in the coming years. Equipment is the most stable of the items on the list, while a drop in spending on transports, alcohol and tobacco, clothing, hotel/restaurants, and education is expected by 2025. The spending of over 60s clearly focuses on quality of life and well-being, as they set aside more frivolous pleasures like smoking or obsessive clothes shopping in favor of spending on experiences, social life, and good quality food (Figure 4.2). Even travel suffers a decrease as aging people gradually lose the desire to travel and discover new places, especially if distant, preferring to fully enjoy the community of which they are already part. Attention to these trends is very important to drive intelligent investment.

Having provided a snapshot of the current situation, we now shift to considering opportunities that could emerge in the coming years. These phenomena

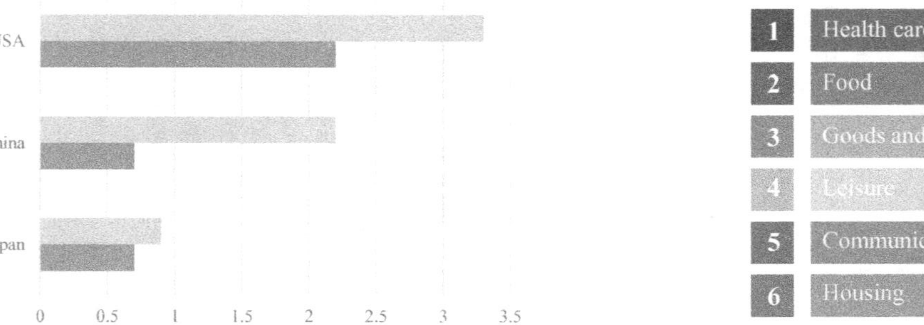

Middle and **high-class** citizens **spending** in the top 3 countries.

The **top 6 purchasing items** by private citizens.

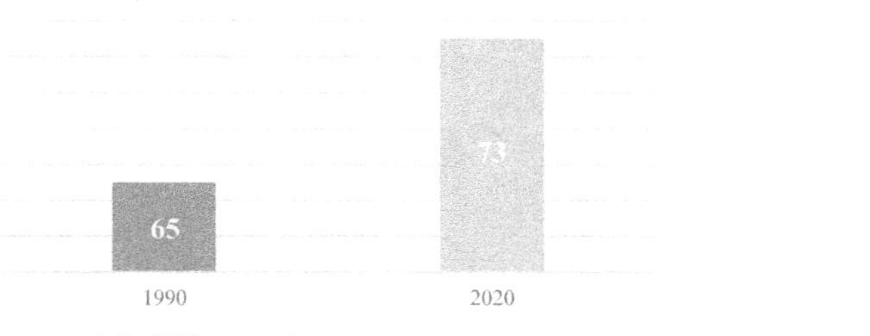

The average **global life expectancy**.

Life expectancy in Europe, US, Latin America.

Figure 4.2 Demographics and private spending

Source: Rothschild & Co. (2023), Thematic Insight: the Silver Economy, with own edits

have already started in some areas of the globe, while they are lagging in others, and more information is needed to know how to best direct investment.

- **Silverization of sectors**: The "silverization of sectors" refers to the growing trend of the silver economy spreading throughout various sectors of the economy, just like an epidemic. The increasing population rate of senior citizens means a growing potential pool of users. Companies that attend to this trend as soon as possible will have more time to plan a winning strategy and conquer the market.
- **New arising professions**: Similar to products/services, the professions related to senior and elder care may undergo changes. Responding to new needs that will emerge should encourage the emergence of new professions with different vertical skills that are currently lacking today.
- **Public spending**: Inevitably, public spending for services for senior citizens will also increase as their numbers increase. Although the private sector is the first to respond to profit from this shift, every government will also have to bear costs that it can afford to ignore today.
- **Entertainment**: As people age, their free time increases and their spending capacity is usually higher than other age groups. The desire to fill leisure time with entertainment will increase the need for services/products designed for this specific age target, opening the door to new players on the market.
- **West vs. East**: As already shown, China registered the highest projected rate of expenditure relative to the characteristics of its population. However, it is not the only Eastern country that deserves attention. As the World Data Lab article mentioned, other countries like Bangladesh, India, Laos, Myanmar, and Vietnam may experience an 80% increase in spending power per capita (World Data Lab, 2019). So, despite the fact that the West gets the most attention given the huge possibilities, things could change in the coming decades.
- **Re-launching economies**: It is good to remember that the growth of the silver economy could benefit many companies and create many jobs. Countries such as Italy and Japan, for example, given the characteristics of their population, should be particularly interested in understanding the phenomenon and investing in it. This sector could be a lever on which to balance their economies.

Having identified the most interesting upcoming opportunities from a purely economic point of view, we must not forget the strong links with the technological sphere. In fact, many of the nascent businesses will have a rather high technological rate. Advances in terms of both product and service through forthcoming innovations will have a potentially remarkable ability to integrate with market needs and meet customers' needs. Here, we have isolated three points of particular interest that will be addressed in the remainder of this chapter.

Gerontechnology: According to the National Center of Biotechnology Information (Chen, L. K., 2020):

> Gerontechnology is defined as an interdisciplinary field linking existing and developing technologies to the aspirations and needs of aging and aged adults. Gerontechnology supports 'successful aging' and is a response to the combination of the aging of society and rapidly emerging new technologies.

Based on this definition, the use of both robotics and AI (the final two points of interest) to support successful aging falls under Gerontechnology. Within the development process of any new ground-breaking product, cutting-edge technology, or better-tailored service, the "co-design" phase is critical. This involves the participation of end users in the creation of a certain product or service with an important level of innovation. Participation is usually requested by the manufacturer, and eligible subjects are selected from those who volunteer. Specific working groups are then formed and divided by subject area, features to be implemented, or any other metric chosen by the company. The contribution of users is essential to help a company understand which aspects to pay particular attention to and, in the case of tight deadlines, create a hierarchy of attributes, features, and/or objects to prioritize. To support open innovation, these same subjects can provide and discuss their point of view, participating in innovation by providing an external reading key. In the past, little attention was paid to seniors' participation in such co-design processes; however, given the growing needs related to the silver economy, that paradigm has now changed. Therefore, seniors' contribution in the design phase of products/services targeted specifically for customers in their age demographic is of fundamental importance. One example of applying the co-design principle in Gerontechnology is the Galilee Medical Center's experiment involving over 65 Israeli subjects in the development and testing of an app for recording and preventing falls. Called Age TechCare, the app is available for both smartphones and smart TVs and demonstrates the importance of seniors' contributions to products and services designed for them (Mazuz & Biswas, 2022).

Robotics is a closely linked field that involves the use of robots to serve end users by helping them carry out even the smallest daily actions. Unlike other fields of application of robotics, robotics' most useful contributions in the context of the silver economy are smaller gestures. An elderly person who lives alone, for example, may have a huge difficulty reaching shelves that are too high or objects on the floor that are too low. Or, they may struggle to navigate stairs. In such situations, help with the small gestures of everyday life can make all the difference. It follows that the level of machines' technological sophistication must be adjusted accordingly.

Among the various countries that are already developing innovative robotic solutions, we can include Japan. As described in a *Financial Times* article, the development of the robotics sector in Japan will, on the one hand, serve to ensure greater independence and autonomy among the elderly, and, on the other hand, give a boost to this sector of the economy (Soble, 2014). Additionally, there will be increasing involvement of robots in person-related services, which are usually performed by a caregiver or nurse. Such machines can off 24-hour, 7-days-a-week monitoring or help nurses on call to carry out their work. Given their potential, robots definitely represent a step forward for both personal care and economic growth in countries with aging populations.

An essential element that has greatly improved the field of robotics, just like other technological fields, is the development of artificial intelligence. In the broad sense of the term, we can define AI as machines' autonomous ability to learn, synthesize, report, and carry out more or less complex functions. After a first phase of training that involves instructing the machine by providing certain inputs, it will gradually be able to begin performing one or more functions consistently with the inputs provided. As the machine is trained with an ever-increasing amount of data and the training phase is extended over a sufficient span of time, the machine will be able to perform increasingly complex functions with an ever-increasing degree of autonomy. Although the logic underlying the development of each AI is almost identical, the fields of application are countless.

Limiting our treatment of this topic to the context of the silver economy, a first observation must be made regarding the "datafication of aging", which refers to the large amount of data that will be produced in the years to come involving a whole series of bodily parameters that will be used in medical evaluations and other activities related to the world of wellness. For example, data about the state of one's heart health, blood pressure, assimilation of macro and micronutrients, and more can be very useful for both trainers and nutritionists who design diets and training plans to optimize results and ensure greater longevity. Having a lot of data available in this field can also mean having a significant database with which to instruct the AI of a hypothetical fitness and nutrition app so that it could become capable of developing an effective training and nutrition plan. Therefore, having more data is certainly a plus at a general level.

In this specific context, it would also be interesting to study the sociological aspect in relation to the technological one. Indeed, the very way that older people are dependent on new technologies is changing and will change more and more in the decades to come. As already written, companies are increasingly including the elderly in the co-design phase of products for which they are targets, and studies based on this work have already been carried out, as shown in an article in *Frontiers* (Gallistl et al., 2023). Another field of AI application that is very close to robotics is nursing technologies. Having a machine that can physically help a nurse or a caregiver provide care for an elderly person is certainly convenient. Having an intelligent machine that can perform certain functions independently is a remarkable plus. For example, a robot that is able to constantly monitor the intake of medicines by the elderly and know how to provide the right doses with proper timing would greatly improve the autonomy of the elderly and facilitate the assistance of authorized personnel. Thus, AI can effectively support the entire eHealth scope. In other words, increasingly smart technologies can improve the provision of health and care services.

Considering the role of increasingly smart technologies, we can also mention the field of wearables among the sectors that deserve attention. In fact, increasingly more technological and intelligent fabrics are being developed that combine good usability in terms of material and comfort with intelligence offered by the insertion of micro and nanotechnologies inside fabrics. The goal of this line of products, which to date remain only prototypes, is to capture as much information related to a person's physical parameters as possible and send this data to a physical/cloud data center for management and security. From there, they can contribute to safeguarding the wearer's well-being. Obviously, we are talking about a complex issue that intersects with legal issues regarding data protection and cyber-attacks. Thus, we are less enthusiastic about business opportunities for smart clothes because risk management is complex and requires time and investment; nevertheless, this is undoubtedly the path many enterprises want to take in the future, and it includes not only smart clothes, but also smart devices more generally.

Indeed, everything that falls within the perimeter of the Internet of Things (IoT) will play an increasingly important role in monitoring, reporting, and analyzing body data. For example, smartwatches are a category of consumer product that, among the many features offered, can also monitor the user's heartbeat and detect any abnormalities. The data on the smartwatch can then be transferred to a smartphone to present a clearer and more readable graphical interface. To this combination of smart devices could also be added 3D virtual reality headsets that allow wearers to practice sports using one of the many sport gamification programs that are spreading among consumers. In short, IoT includes a wide range of increasingly interconnected and smart devices.

Finally, as mentioned in one of the articles edited by the famous Spanish bank Banco Santander, it is important to address the aspect related to the Banking of Things (BoT) (Santander, 2022). Just as IoT describes the connectivity between various devices capable of managing, analyzing, and exchanging data and information by exploiting an available internet network without any distinction between specific product or service, BoT is specific to all those banking-related products, offers, and services that are delivered to the customer in a smarter way and that have improving the quality of banking and insurance services as their main objective. Thus, it is correct to define BoT as an IoT sub-set that intentionally exploits the technological advancements brought by IoT to improve and streamline the supply of banking and insurance services to clients. A couple of significant examples of the practical applications of BoT in an everyday activity are described in the Santander (2022) article:

> For instance, picture an Internet-connected washing machine that can order detergent from a supermarket or online store when it's running low. For that, it would need a virtual wallet with sufficient funds or a registered bank card. An electronic device that could administer its own spare parts, replenish products or notify the manufacturer of the need for a replacement at the end of its shelf life would become a point of sale.

Lastly, Figure 4.3 summarizes the main concepts that were addressed in the above analysis of the technological components of the silver economy, clearly and visually representing the underlying technological framework.

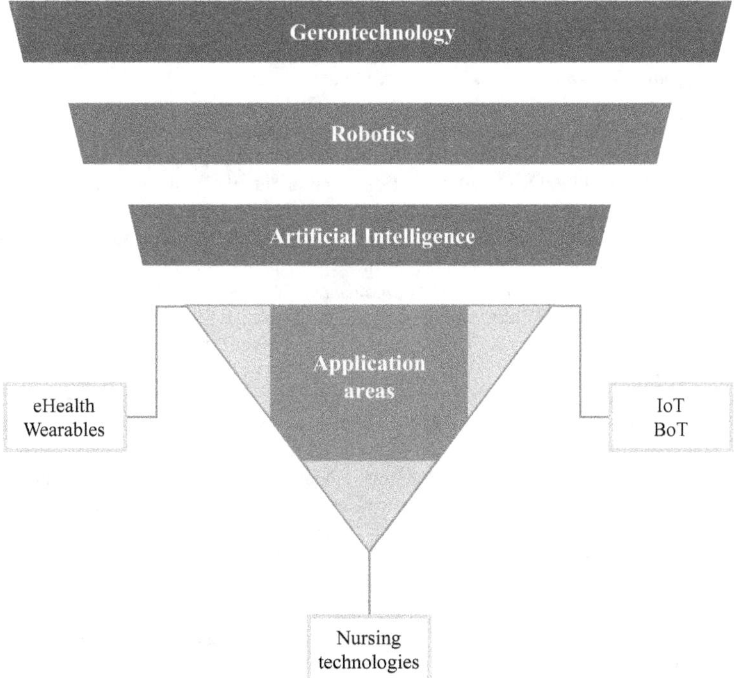

Figure 4.3 The technological funnel of the Silver Economy

Source: Own source and edits

References

Bennet, M., & James, P. (1999). *Key themes in environmental, social and sustainability performance evaluation and reporting*. In James, B. M. (Ed.), *Sustainable measures. Evaluation and reporting of environmental and social performance*. Sheffield: Greenleaf Publishing, pp 29–74.

Boston Consulting Group (2022). *The strategic race to sustainability*. Available at the following link: https://www.bcg.com/publications/2022/winning-strategic-race-to-sustainability

Commission of the European Communities (2002). *Comunicazione della Commissione relativa alla responsabilità sociale delle imprese: un contributo delle imprese allo sviluppo sostenibile*. Bruxelles. Available at the following link: https://eur-lex.europa.eu/LexUriServ/LexUriServ.do?uri=COM:2002:0347:FIN:it:PDF

Chen, L. K. (2020). Gerontechnology and artificial intelligence: Better care for older people. *Archives of gerontology and geriatrics*, *91*, 104252.

Doyle, M. W., & Stiglitz, J. E. (2014). Eliminating extreme inequality: A sustainable development goal, 2015–2030. *Ethics & International Affairs*, *28*(1), 5–13.

Elkington, J. (2007). *Triple bottom line*. In Visser, W., Matten, D., Pohl, M., & Tolhurst, N. (Eds.), *The A to Z of corporate social responsibility* (pp. 465–466). Sussex: John Wiley and Sons, Ltd.

Fengler, W. (2021). *The silver economy is coming of age: A look at the growing spending power of seniors*. Brookings, United States of America.

Gallistl, V., Katz, S., Kolland, F., & Peine, A. (2023). Socio-gerontechnology—New perspectives on the digital transformation of later life. *Frontiers in Sociology*, *8*, 1183572.

Gazzola, P., & Colombo, G. (2014). CRS integration into the corporate strategy. *Cross Cultural Management Journal*, *16*(2), 331–338.

Gazzola, P., Grechi, D., Ossola, P., & Pavione, E. (2019). Certified Benefit Corporations as a new way to make sustainable business: The Italian example. *Corporate Social Responsibility and Environmental Management*, *26*(6), 1435–1445.

Griggs, D., Stafford-Smith, M., Gaffney, O., Rockström, J., Öhman, M. C., Shyamsundar, P., & Noble, I. (2013). Policy: Sustainable development goals for people and planet. *Nature*, *495*(7441), 305.

Iberdrola, Silver Economy (2023). Older people will be the engine of the economy of the future. Available at the following link: https://www.iberdrola.com/innovation/silver-economy

Lee, B. X., Kjaerulf, F., Turner, S., Cohen, L., Donnelly, P. D., Muggah, R., & Waller, I. (2016). Transforming our world: implementing the 2030 agenda through sustainable development goal indicators. *Journal of Public Health Policy*, *37*(1), 13–31.

Magee, L., Scerri, A., James, P., Thom, J. A., Padgham, L., Hickmott, S., & Cahill, F. (2013). Reframing social sustainability reporting: Towards an engaged approach. *Environment, Development and Sustainability*, *15*(1), 225–243.

Mazuz, K., & Biswas, S. (2022). Co-designing technology and aging in a service setting: Developing an interpretive framework of how to interact with older age users. *Gerontechnology*, *21*(1), 1–13.

Meyer, J. L., & Helfman, G. S. (1993). The ecological basis of sustainability. *Ecological Applications*, *3*(4), 569–571.

Porter, M. E., & Kramer, M. R. (2002). The competitive advantage of corporate philanthropy. *Harvard Business Review*, *80*(12), 56–68.

Rothschild & Co. (2023). *Thematic insight: The silver economy*. Available at the following link: https://www.rothschildandco.com/en/newsroom/insights/2023/01/thematic-insights-the-silver-economy/

Ruggiero, A., & Fatigati, T. (2021). Tendenze Nuove, 2, 1–6.

Ruggiero, A., & Fatigati, T. (2022). Silver economy & technology. *Tendenze Nuove*, 2, 1–6.

Santander (2022). Banking of things: What is it? Available at the following link: https://www.santander.com/en/stories/banking-of-things-what-is-it

Soble, J. (2014). The Silver Economy: Japan embraces the future of robot care. *Financial Times*. Available at the following link: https://www.ft.com/content/cdb0dbe8-292b-11e4-8b81-00144feabdc0

Technopolis Group, Oxford Economics (2018). *The Silver Economy*. European Commission. Available at the following link: http://publications.europa.eu/resource/cellar/2dca9276-3ec5-11e8-b5fe-01aa75ed71a1.0002.01/DOC_1

United Nations (2015). Transforming our world: The 2030 Agenda for sustainable development. Available at the following link: https://sustainabledevelopment.un.org/post2015/transformingourworld/publication

World Data Lab (2019). Silver economy spending power trends in Asia. Available at the following link: https://worlddata.io/silver-economy-spending-power-trends-in-asia/

5 Technology

How it is shaping the future of wellness

5.1 Introduction

The driver that is influencing all economic activities is the technological dimension or, more generally, innovation, the term used to refer to the translation of a new idea, scientific development, or technological achievement into a new product or production process (Foster & Kaplan, 2001). In the conventional view, which takes its cue from Schumpeter's contribution (Schumpeter, 1935), innovation is essentially technological and radical—i.e., a change that marks a break with the past, a sort of leap that leads to an advantage of cost, quality, or performance. Over time, changes in the environmental context and, consequently, approaches in the literature on the subject have revised the concept of innovation, re-evaluating the importance of incremental improvements (Freeman, 1974). Since the 1990s, innovation studies have been gradually enriched with new contributions, initiating a process of progressive integration of the radical and incremental approaches and elaborating articulated models that consider a plurality of both internal and external factors (Cooper & Kleinschmidt, 1988).

Despite many definitions of technology existing across the most disparate academic fields, here we only address the definition of technology in a purely business context. Within this perimeter, we can define technology as both a software and a hardware phenomenon (Harmondsworth Meyer & Helfman,1993). On the software side, it enables research and the development of new programs capable of performing certain tasks that will benefit business activities. An example in this respect is the use of in-house R&D to implement a particularly complex and advanced AI capable of performing important tasks. Think of the recent comparison between the Optimus robot developed by Tesla's research centers in the USA and another robot model called Atlas developed by Boston Dynamics. The first model has a much lower intelligence than Atlas, which suggests that the AI software development is very different between the companies being compared. If the former is only suitable for performing "elementary" tasks and making simple gestures, the latter model is capable of jumping, running, and recognizing the surrounding space. This example is masterly for understanding how

DOI: 10.4324/9781003475699-6

impactful and diverse the development of an AI can be. On the hardware side, a technological advancement may lead to the discovery of new and more suitable construction materials for manufacturing a certain product, an improved design, or a more generalist or, conversely, an extremely specialized field of application, depending on requirements. In this case, technology manifests in a physical improvement of the product. Ultimately, the materials used to manufacture Tesla's Optimus and Boston Dynamics' Atlas are different because the final products are different in terms of properties, technological advancement, and skills. The Optimus is designed to perform actions that help customers in small repetitive everyday gestures, and the price is deliberately low to allow for mass market purchasing. Atlas, however, is designed for high performance, demanding tasks, even in a war context, so the quality of the materials is noticeably different. Therefore, the price is similarly intended for large buyers who can afford this expense, such as a nation interested in modernizing its army by purchasing robot soldiers.

Comparably, technological advances in the wellness industry, generally, and the fitness market, more specifically, involve products and services designed for a large audience, where the rate of technological advancement is secondary to other parameters. In other cases, when products' core is represented by the particularities of their materials rather than the vastness of their functions, their level of sophistication depends on the target customer and their needs. The big difference that is becoming increasingly evident, however, is that compared to the past, where well-being passed through the attendance of a physical place, now the world of wellness is entering our homes through the powerful tool of technology. For this reason, related to both health and the logic of the market, technological advancement plays a primary role, because it allows companies to reach the final consumer in places and ways that were previously unthinkable. Given these peculiarities, this chapter will consider the effects that the development of technology is having on sectoral dynamics.

5.2 Technology as a disruptor and value creator

According to a 2021 report by the well-known consulting firm Bain & Company, technology is regarded as "the primary disruptor and value creator across all sectors" (Crawford, 2021). This is because the technological factor enables the acquisition of increasing market shares and, therefore, is the main determinant of entrepreneurial success in every market. In fact, from 2015 to 2020, less tech-oriented companies made fewer gains in comparison to their more technologically oriented competitors. The advantages are even more pronounced for those so-called "born tech" companies that had bet on technology as the key to their success from day one. Time has rewarded them. Tesla, for example, is worth more than other historic and iconic brands that have been on the market for over a century. This trend has become so clear that even famous "brick and mortar" businesses are implementing tech-oriented strategies. To conceive of this impact one only has to think of how all prestigious supermarket chains now offer online shopping service with home delivery. Therefore, regardless of whether a business originated as digital or physical, the digitization of the business is no longer an option but a fundamental lever to compete effectively and improve market share.

While the generalized need to digitize is clear, understanding how to do it is much more difficult. Effectively managing the implementation of a digitization project for the development of a specific software, functionality, or process engineering improvement is no simple matter. The winners of this technology trend are cloud technologies and platform businesses. Companies that are able to offer this business model as part of their value proposition are able to generate impressive customer acquisition and retention and grind out profits. Bain & Company's 2021 survey shows the market value of the Top-20 companies in each included sector and concludes that the less technological they are, the less competitive they are. The report emphasizes the undisputed leadership of the so-called "hyperscalers", such as Apple, Microsoft, and Amazon, and focuses on cloud-native infrastructure software vendors. Although the latter have been overshadowed by the performance and fame of the hyperscalers, all of these companies have the highest value and have demonstrated their ability to win the market and to achieve astonishing results. This has not gone unnoticed in the eyes of investors, who have rewarded the stocks. In fact, collectively, the companies mentioned in the report had reached an ambitious half-trillion-dollar value by the end of 2020, with many seeing their market value double the following year. A growing list of "unicorns" is also rising above the crowd.

Companies based on cloud services have the advantage of not having to worry about heavy upfront costs, as they have the option of paying for the cloud storage, security, and speed service based on actual usage traffic. Thus, while higher usage leads to higher expenses, it is reasonable to assume that higher utilization is the result of greater sales, so higher costs also represent higher revenues. This mechanism enables all cloud-based businesses to avoid going into debt for upfront costs. Instead, they can concentrate on using their resources well to focus on business growth, strategic positioning, competitiveness, sales, marketing, and customer care. It is precisely in cloud services that many "platform businesses" have their roots. Thanks to the available servers, generated data traffic, peak management, security, guaranteed speed, and other sophisticated services, platform businesses are the "coolest" business models of the moment.

Generally speaking, we can say that a platform business is a business model capable of generating exponential returns depending on the number of companies it manages to involve in its business. For example, the current profitability of Apple, which has a very strong brand and a stellar market value, is not because iPhone or the new Mac sales, but because of all the services and accessories connected to these devices. Behind an Apple product like an iPhone, for example, there is turnover involving more than 80 different companies. It is precisely this ability to involve other companies in its business that makes Apple so profitable. Therefore, to define it merely as an electronics company is completely reductive. Another distinctive feature of platform businesses is their ability to connect the consumer side with the developer side. Creating a platform means connecting these two sides so that they can exchange value within that environment. Developers need the platform because it is a market populated by consumers interested in a certain product and already clustered in some way. On the user side, platforms are indispensable as places where desired goods/services can be found and acquired. If a traditional business based on the pipeline model has proven to be able to generate incremental returns, a platform business can generate exponential returns. For example, Apple's famous App Store has become increasingly valuable over the years because it is a marketplace that connects the user side with the service developer side. It is the only marketplace where it is legal to buy/sell software that works on Apple systems, which are notoriously "closed" by strategic choice, so there are no alternatives. Control of the App Store also indirectly supports the management of all related software companies that aim to sell their apps to potential customers there. This supply/demand match creates a real ecosystem of companies interested in interacting directly with the customer to pivot their product/service and eventually scale up. In such a business model, revenues can potentially rise quickly. Once again, all this is possible thanks to cloud infrastructures.

Mergers and acquisitions (M&A) represent another related topic. Indeed, many players in the tech industry, such as Google or Microsoft, have engaged in aggressive takeover policies that still persist today. Obviously, from their point of view, these are moves dictated by market contingencies. There is important potential in certain startups that they want to try to seize through an acquisition before the startup can grow, scale, and become more or less direct and dangerous competitors. As mentioned earlier, platform businesses have exponential growth potential, so what is just a small but promising tech startup today could become "the next big thing" tomorrow, competing directly with the big players that exist today. As a preventive strategy, therefore, well-established companies now engage in "scouting", and once they have identified a promising startup that has proven it can create market-proven value and is ready to scale, they come in and make a favorable takeover offer with a twofold purpose: to nip a potential competitor in the bud and to help the tech startup grow and continue to garner revenues once it becomes part of the group's portfolio of companies. In doing so, these Big Tech players become bigger and bigger, increasingly consolidating their dominant position in the market and becoming exponentially more profitable.

Many have questioned and continue to question the lawfulness of this market practice. The relevant supervisory authorities always observe these initiatives suspiciously, and it is no coincidence that some acquisitions are temporary blocked due to the imposition of new policies, especially in Europe. Only after an often lengthy series of checks and due diligence is the operation eventually resumed. Much of the skepticism of these finance operations is dictated by a subjective and suspicious view than by objective evidence. Fear of possible market abuse prevails over economic research. However, economic research seems to suggest that such more or less "aggressive" market moves ultimately benefit consumers and do not hinder market competitiveness. In particular, Bain & Co.'s 2021 analysis looked at acquisitions by the Top-5 US "hyperscalers" (Alphabet, Amazon, Apple, Facebook and Microsoft) that took place from 2015 to 2020. It covered acquisitions worth $300 million and above, totaling $150 billion over the time frame. This analysis found that acquisitions during that period created benefits for consumers without compromising competitiveness within the market.

Another sign of the importance of having technology assets within one's business plan is the enormous value that venture capitalists (VCs) assign these types of startups, even doubling the funds invested. It could be argued that the technology push brought about by these tech-oriented companies has been fostered and pushed by VCs. In fact most of the funds received by tech startups from 2010 to 2020 are the result of agreements made with VCs and corporate venture capitalists (CVCs). While VCs and CVCs investments in tech startups fell by 13% between 2018 and 2020, the COVID-19 pandemic crisis and related socio-political implications made investors refocus their attention on this type of startup, so the market has started to grow again.

The focus is now on more "mature" startups as opposed to those in the seed or startup phase. In other words, rather than launching into small companies that do not yet have an MVP, have not adequately tested the market, or have not taken the "crossing the chasm" step, investors now tend to invest in more "later stage" startups, i.e., those that have reached a funding round C or higher. In fact, the same report shows an incredible +165% for the first quarter of 2021 compared to the same period the year before. Thus, the direction taken by VCs and CVCs is clear. While this move can be seen as a choice on the part of investors to continue investing in potentially profitable ventures without taking too many risks, thus avoiding startups that are too "young" and not yet "validated by the market", startups also prefer private investments rather than going public and being subject to the constraint of profitability at all costs, with increasingly stringent deadlines to meet.

Finally, to add a final level of detail when discussing the importance of technology in startups, it is worth considering that the most profitable are precisely those startups based on a strong artificial intelligence (AI) and machine learning (ML) development component. Since many sectors are now based on the massive use of AI and ML, start-ups capable of integrating these capabilities into their business models manage to impress more and, thus, receive more funding. Although the product/service offered may be very specific, a good AI and ML component behind it allows investors to think about the possibility expanding its scope to have cross-industry relevance. At the level of investments by geographical area, the two dominant countries, by far, are the USA and China.

5.3 The digitalization of wellness: between customer satisfaction and technological complexity

Everyone from passionate amateurs to professionals is now watching the rapid and progressive digitalization of the wellness industry. This radical transformation is embracing both products and services related to this industry (Arizton, 2023). As for products, just think of the gym machines that are undergoing an evolution not only from a mechanical point of view but also electronically, integrating the internet into the machinery's various functions. For example, a treadmill has gone from being a purely mechanical object with only one function to offering new pre-selected running paths and simulating individual races. Today, it is even possible to connect to the internet and participate in virtual classes with a coach and other athletes committed to following a path selected by the trainer and shared with all participants via the internet, with the possibility of monitoring each participant's performance and effort. This last aspect has allowed machines designed for training at home to give the end user the perception of begin engaged in a collective activity carried out remotely. That's why other objects particularly suitable for sports activities at home, such as elastic bands or yoga mats, do not preclude amateurs from training at home alone but being connected with other participants via the internet. Thanks to incredible scientific advances, even a simple object like a yoga mat can contain sensors that collect a series of data and physical parameters and connect with a dedicated app to monitor the correct execution of the exercise.

As previously stated, the services section has not gone unaddressed either. In fact, where the physical presence of a reference figure used to be required to give advice, instructions, suggestions, or corrections, all of this support can happen remotely without losing quality and effectiveness. For example, a newbie who wants to go to the gym for the first time and get the help of a competent trainer who is qualified to create training schedules can now rely on live video and document sharing via the internet. It is no longer strange to physically go to a gym in any given city and be supported by a coach who lives anywhere in the world and joins via the internet. This argument is as valid for all other services related to people's well-being and health as it is for improving physical performance, so it is possible to imagine telehealth consultations with medical experts, nutritionists, sleep experts, and so on (Businesswire, 2023). The potential applications of technology in this industry and the enormous advantages of those applications for end users should be clear. Access to the world of fitness and to personal care more generally has been greatly facilitated by such applications, allowing people to increase the healthy habit of physical activity, which has been seriously threatened by the bad habits of modern society. In addition, such applications enable people to measure their overall health level more effectively than before, ultimately improving longevity. However, we must also consider the complexity that this world of countless integrations brings with it. After all, not everything that shines is gold.

The first significant shortcoming is lack of internet connectivity. Access to the internet enables home automation that can help with even the smallest daily activities, which is made possible by digital tools and devices being connected to each other through an internet connection. Alternatively, smartphones offer access to an endless array of information. Smartphones cannot store all of the information they offer access to. Therefore, although it is often taken for granted today, we must never forget that this critical service is made available by companies operating in the TLC sector, whose core business consists precisely in providing the fastest and most efficient network system possible to as many people as possible, even those living in rural areas that are difficult to reach. Just like any service, it is subject to interruptions for different reasons (ordinary and extraordinary maintenance, weather events, disrepair, etc.). Therefore, to rely on digital technology by exploiting the connectivity between various devices and machines always implies a good quality of incoming/outgoing data traffic, as there is a strong dependence with the network provider.

Moreover, as all of this data traffic is transmitted on the web, there are also cybersecurity implications to consider. Data protection is a topic of public debate, both for the protection of corporate digital assets and for private individuals. We must also evaluate the protocols for protecting data transmitted live and stored in various databases. While it is true that training data are not classified as highly compromising, if we extend the perimeter to considering wellness in general, we can understand the importance of data protection related to body parameters, ongoing and past diseases, current treatments, etc. This second category of data is classifiable as sensitive and deserves maximum security. Every time someone accesses an internet network, they not only access an almost unlimited network of information, but they can also open a backdoor to possible hacker attacks and data breaches. Since such attacks multiplied during the COVID period, especially for some types of companies, it is good to keep this aspect in mind and not underestimate its importance.

The digitalization of wellness is divided into two major areas of attention: the countless advantages for the consumer and the great attention that must be put into the management and treatment of each individual's confidential data (Euromonitor International, 2022). Below, the main points of emphasis for each of these areas is addressed though the two macro-categories of *business* and *IT*.

Business:

- **Diversified offering**: While there used to only be one type of value proposal based on physical presence in a specific place, the concept of materiality has now lost that value, as a product/service can be usable even at a distance. Trainers can remotely guide and observe many workouts, and advice on nutrition, integration, or sleep even is available simply by accessing an app or website. Neither effectiveness nor results are compromised. In the wellness field, different exercises or treatments can be carried out independently with or without someone's supervision. Moreover, through access to online classes, users can overcome feelings of isolation by training in the company of others but remaining in the comfort of their own homes. Therefore, while acknowledging the irreplaceable importance of physical presence for certain activities, such as a professional physical examination or team training, many aspects related to the ordinary care of people's well-being can be facilitated digitally. Neither the trend of sports lovers who continued to train in a mixed home/gym mode: even after COVID nor the growth of apps providing home workouts should be a surprise.
- **Cost savings**: The savings aspect should also not be underestimated. In fact, where the choice of a product/service used to be linked to the geographical area of reference, the expansion of markets and the efficiency of logistics systems have made it possible to buy goods and services from producers who are located anywhere. Wellness is also experiencing a considerable upgrade. While the number of experts in the field was quite limited in the past, it no longer is. There are many professionals with diverse skills that can better fit different individual's goals. The ease of getting in touch with experts from around the world has also made prices more competitive. From the point of view of the final consumer, however, this has resulted in a greater chance to seize the most affordable offer and save money.
- **Time reduction**: Another aspect is related to the difficulty of moving between one place and another, resulting in increased time transportation costs. When professional consultations had to be held face-to-face, the possibility of finding available time was limited. It is not always possible to take time off from work to reach a certain place, especially if it is far from one's place of residence or work. This is definitely a daunting factor for those who want to take care of themselves. The ease of access to services related to wellness, without taking up too much time in a day, is important. For this reason, the digitization of most services has encouraged consumers to approach a healthy lifestyle more calmly, without taking too much time from other daily activities.
- **More touchpoints with clients**: One of the most important aspects to get to potential customers involves contact and communication strategies.

The greater the number of potential customers involved in the presentation of a product/service, the greater the number of conversions into paying customers. Therefore, the number of customer communication channels is also important and must be managed with care. Thanks to the creation of numerous websites and dedicated apps related to the sphere of wellness, the roads through which companies can reach potential consumers are dramatically increasing. Thus, many companies in the industry have tried to embrace digitization to boost sales. Digital channels are also an opportunity for companies to diversify their value proposition. Online content that is better suited to remote use can be created alongside the maintenance of a physical offer, making it even more attractive in the eyes of the final consumer. This means that digital channels can complement physical channels and improve the marketing mix to increase sales.

- **Customer Relationship Management (CRM)**: Nowadays, a handshake is not enough to establish a lasting relationship with customers; it requires much more attention than before. The globalization of markets has increased companies' competitiveness, and the battle to win customers has become even more fierce. Thus, the focus on the sales processes has increased accordingly. Today, in fact, the various stages of sales are attended by specialized figures. One of these phases deals precisely with developing lasting customer relationships through after-sales communication strategies. This effort involves analyzing and interpreting a large amount of data associated with the product in relation to the customer, trying to maximize the utility for the customer. Amazon has schooled the market in this sense, teaching everyone that the best way to be competitive is to be completely disinterested in competitors and their strategies while maintaining maximum and constant attention on their customers. This data-driven approach is not limited to Big Tech; it also influences other industries, including wellness. The large amount of data that users share with companies allows those businesses to understand a lot of user usage habits, and based on this data, they try to diversify offers according to the needs that emerge. Then, based on the data of the use of a product/service by the individual user, they create better versions of the same. For example, the data transmitted to Fitbit in the daily use of its smartwatches can help the company understand which areas can be improved, perhaps by inserting a more accurate calories burned tracker for the running activity or measuring quality sleeping hours more accurately.
- **Social media as new advertising**: The advertising sector has evolved over the decades, especially since the 1950s, experimenting with increasingly faster developments. Today, we could say that the frontier of experimentation in this field are the advertising campaigns in the Metaverse, a virtual environment that presents many logics typical of the physical world. Several brands have already purchased spaces within the Metaverse in which

to advertise the new releases of their products/services. However, this form of advertising is still marginal compared to much more widespread advertising through social media channels. Anyone who uses a social platform—and billions of users have more than one—can take advantage of the online store section in the App. This is because the platforms themselves, which started as simple spaces for sharing personal content, have become increasingly commercial, and today they are real showcases for getting products/ services in front of the public. As a result, influencers, the protagonists who sponsor the products/services offered to their audience, have become the sellers of today. The audiences that follow these personalities can easily be cross-generational; therefore, the pool of potential customers is considerable. Depending on their content, influencers can access a cluster of specific customers. There are influencers capable of bringing content to a generalist audience, and there are influencers who focus on a narrow niche. This variety offers companies a vast choice in terms of targeting one cluster rather than another. Here, then, apps that were born as a space for socialization between individuals can now become real e-commerce sites. For example, Instagram has evolved from showing simple personal content to becoming a showroom for any type of brand, and this change is important. Moreover, it has happened without ever undermining the user experience; on the contrary, it has enriched it. Today, therefore, users can enjoy both forms of content: a space for sharing memories, like a kind of digital album, and an e-commerce site where users can buy products and services with a few simple steps.

Information Technology (IT) side:

- **Data storage, protection and backup**: When using a "smart" product, which is one equipped with the ability to detect certain parameters and share the collected data for specific application, it is easy to overlook the complexity of safely managing and transmitting the data. Every bit collected due to a hacker attack on corporate servers, for example, can say something about us. At best, our workouts, progressions of strength, endurance, elasticity, and other parameters might be unwittingly shared; at worst, the data can provide information about our state of health. Therefore, companies are eager to provide maximum data protection within hardware devices, software applications, and even across the path that transmits data from one place to another. This involves understanding where to store the collected data, what the best possible cybersecurity solutions are for protecting the data, and how often to make periodic backups. Passively managing data is no longer enough. Now, we require "active management", i.e., continuous control and monitoring, with the possibility of changing certain settings at any time to obviate any need. So, every time a new smart device that can also be used for sports, such as an Apple watch, is brought to the market, companies are required to carry out a long series of activities related to managing and protecting the data collected. Doing this work requires involving cybersecurity experts and respecting the current regulations, which can also change significantly from country to country.

- **Data integration with third parties:** The services contained in the apps we use daily are downloaded for free or purchased within different marketplaces. Developers who want to place their apps on the market to offer them to potential customers cannot disregard the technical requirements demanded of these marketplaces. The two largest and best known are certainly the Apple App Store and Google Play Store, which contain the market globally. From a computer programming point of view, integrating the functionalities of an application with others means adapting scripts so that all functionality can flow from one app to another without losing data or encountering errors, thus making the user experience as smooth as possible. In this sense, the experience offered by Apple remains the best because Apple devices have a very high level of integration of both hardware and software across products, creating a "closed system" that makes the user experience extremely fluid. However, the Android world offered by Google is still behind because of the number of manufacturers that create products that run the Android operating system. The fewer hardware connections, the faster it is to fix bugs and errors and make improvements to scripts, while the vastness of the Android world, with dozens of brands operating in it, makes the process of third-party integration much slower and more cumbersome, at the expense of the user experience, which can be good, but is not perfectly fluid. These dynamics affect apps of all types, including those related to the wellness sector. For example, from the point of view of a company that develops an at-home training app, the more it can be integrated with various devices, the smoother the user experience will be. This could lead to an increase in user base and, therefore, monetization. In contrast, from an end user's point of view, if an app cannot function across various devices that a person might use, there is a loss of utility, which might cause the user to switch to another service provider, leading to a decrease in the user base and consequent reduction in business revenue. Thus, data integrations between software and hardware are both important from a business point of view and difficult to achieve from a computer science standpoint.
- **Centralized health data management:** The centralized management of health and wellness data is closely related to the importance of user data protection and the integration of third-party apps' functionality. At the level of IT infrastructure, it could be visualized as a kind of "super app" capable of acting as a centralized manager of a large amount of data. Apps already exist that can manage training data, nutrition, sleep, and even a digital medical record. However, tech companies are continuing

to innovate and the creation of an easy-to-use super app, integrated in the various ecosystems, with reliable protection standards, is only a matter of time. Centralized management not only would allow users to monitor progress and habits but also would facilitate the work of the doctors by providing a single space to access the information they need to make a diagnosis much faster and more effectively than in the past. Thus, from a conceptual point of view, a super app could mean a simple solution for handling complex problems. At the business level, an app that condenses all of these benefits could definitely be an opportunity for many companies. From an IT standpoint, the complexity of such a sophisticated architecture requires huge investments in terms of budget, time needed for implementation and testing, and highly skilled professionals.

- **Smart gym equipment**: When we talk about gym equipment, we always think of heavy machinery, typically cast iron, that moves in a pre-set way and allows users to carry out a limited set of exercises. The tools were originally designed to stress specific muscle areas and stimulate the growth of hypertrophy and strength. Over the decades, however, the mechanical component has gradually given way to the electronic component, creating machines capable of performing different training programs. Finally, with the advent of digitalization, machines are able to connect with each other, leading to the creation of live training classes (Egym, 2023). The digital component, therefore, has made increasingly "smart" machinery, unlocking new features. The increasingly sophisticated methods of engineering applied to these types of tools and machinery have also unlocked additional functionality (Lexology, 2019). For instance, there are dumbbells that can change weight depending on the settings, practical and comfortable multi-functional machines that allow you to perform a large number of exercises in a small space, and training balls that can also serve as ergonomic chairs. In particular, it is worth mentioning the innovative, multi-functional Sintesi machine, produced by the Italian startup Akuis, which is able to exploit electromagnetic motors to modulate weight and resistance levels, simulating an entire gym rack in very little space, so it can be used safely at home. In short, the world of fitness equipment is becoming more practical, functional, beautiful in terms of design, and smart.
- **Wireless Body Area Networks (WBANs)**: The new frontier of the sportswear sector is represented by "smart clothes", which are fabrics that contain sensors capable of integrating perfectly into the fabric without losing functionality (Ghent University, 2023). This allows athletes to wear them without noticing any difference in terms of fit and design compared to traditional fabrics, while also detecting and recording a long series of body parameters and data related to their health. Through a highly sophisticated technology, equipped with a series of wireless nodes that connect each other, these fabrics can really be a breakthrough in the wellness industry (Perry, 2023). From a professional standpoint, the ability of a team to

monitor the greatest amount of data related to their athletes is very important, as it can help them understand what to do to make them always perform to the maximum and generate important revenue. But even on an amateur or health level, these fabrics can be an added bonus in personal care. At the amateur level, they can help monitor performance and enable users to understand what to do to increase their performance; at the health level, they can track heart rate at rest and under stress. The most famous sportswear brands in the world, including Nike, Adidas, and Under Armour, are all investing in smart fabrics R&D. These companies were among the first to understand its potential and invest massively in it.

- **Gamification of fitness**: "Gamification" in the fitness field means applying the aspects and dynamics of reward and motivation that are typical of video games to fitness activity to make training fun and motivating rather than boring and tiring (Technogym, 2023). The digital revolution of the video game industry and the high level of engagement that it brought with it motivated this development. It was thought that transposing video game dynamics also to real life sports practices could be a way to motivate athletes. The success of gamification in several areas is now established. Just think of the many gamification mechanisms that exist in the world of work to increase employee performance without additional mental stress or the offers that encourage purchases in order to get points and benefits. Although a solo exercise might seem monotonous, especially when done from home, all of a sudden it might start to seem more engaging and stimulating when it is gamified. These mechanisms are intended to involve the pool of existing customers while, at the same time, potentially reaching new customers. There are now many applications bringing gamification to various areas of sport, including running, cycling, triathlons, and more. Among these, it is certainly worth mentioning Strava, MyCycling, and Skillrow. Another even more sophisticated example is Supernatural, the first service in the world designed for Oculus Quest designed by Meta, then bundled with a virtual reality viewer in 3D, which allows users to train by exploiting all of the potential of augmented reality, recreating exotic environments and exciting games in the comfort of one's home.

After mentioning the six points of attention in reference to the business side and the six related to the IT side, it is useful to conclude by identifying a model with which readers can create a kind of concept map to make these concepts more familiar and easier to use. After reviewing several diagrams, the most adaptable was the so-called Entity Relationship Model or Diagram (ER Model/Diagram). The definition given by the Simplilearn education site is as follows (Ravikiran, 2023):

> An Entity Relationship Diagram is a diagram that represents relationships among entities in a database. It is commonly known as an ER Diagram.

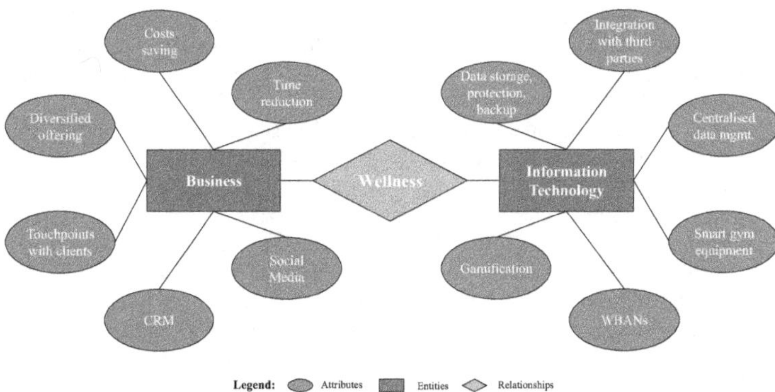

Figure 5.1 Entity Relationship Diagram Model

Source: Own source with own edits

> An ER Diagram in DBMS plays a crucial role in designing the database. Today's business world previews all the requirements demanded by the users in the form of an ER Diagram. Later, it's forwarded to the database administrators to design the database.

As can be seen, the main scope of this model's application is the DBMS (Database Management System), which it describes in terms of the relationships between different entities and attributes. However, using the same symbols but changing reference scope, this scheme adapts well to representing relationships between entities related to both business and IT sides.

Specifically, the symbols used below are:

- **Rectangles** to describe the different types of *entities;*
- **Ellipses** to describe *attributes* belonging to one or more entities; and,
- **Diamonds** to describe the types of *relationships* existing between entities.

Finally, here is a visualization of the ER Model (Figure 5.1):

References

Arizton (2023). Digital health and wellness market - global outlook & forecast 2023–2028. Available at the following link: https://www.arizton.com/market-reports/digital-health-and-wellness-market

Businesswire (2023). Global digital health and wellness market outlook report 2023–2028. Available at the following link: https://www.businesswire.com/news/home/20230421005194/en/Global-Digital-Health-and-Wellness-Market-Outlook-Report-

2023-2028-Increasing-Adoption-of-Telehealth-Data-Analytics-Increasingly-Driving-Wellness-Increasing-Smartphone-Penetration-mhealth---ResearchAndMarkets.com

Cooper, R. G., & Kleinschmidt, E. J. (1988). Resource allocation in the new product process. *Industrial Marketing Management*, *17*(3), 249–262.

Crawford, D. (2021). Technology report, Bain & Company. Available at the following link: https://www.bain.com/insights/welcome-tech-report-2021/

Egym (2023). The impact of digitization and why the fitness industry is next. Available at the following link: https://egym.com/us/blog/digitization-fitness-industry

Euromonitor International (2022). Fostering wellbeing through digitalization and technology. Available at the following link: https://www.euromonitor.com/article/fostering-wellbeing-through-digitalisation-and-technology

Foster, R., & Kaplan, S. (2001). *Creative destruction. Why companies that are built to last underperform the market – And how to successfully transform them*. New York: Random House.

Freeman, C. (1974). The Economics of industrial innovation: Penguin Books. *Ltd., England*, 367.

Ghent University (2023). Wireless Body Area Networks (WBAN). https://www.waves.intec.ugent.be/research/wireless/wbans

Harmondsworth Meyer, J. L., & Helfman, G. S. (1993). The ecological basis of sustainability. *Ecological Applications*, *3*(4), 569–571.

Lexology (2019). How smart is a smart fabric — Does performance apparel deliver on the marketing hype? Available at the following link: https://www.lexology.com/library/detail.aspx?g=d8295a70-ebf4-4daf-bc37-a5fdc4e399d7

Perry, C. (2023). Digital fitness: A new framework for accelerating technology transformation. *Forbes*, May 11, 2023.

Ravikiran, A. S. (2023). ER diagrams in DBMS: Entity Relationship Diagram Model. Simplilearn, May 23, 2023. Available at the following link: https://www.simplilearn.com/tutorials/sql-tutorial/er-diagram-in-dbms

Schumpeter, J. A. (1935). The analysis of economic change. *Review of Economic Statistics*, *17*(4), 1–10.

Technogym (2023). Gamification, o allenarsi divertendosi. Available at the following link: https://www.technogym.com/it/newsroom/gamification-allenarsi-divertendosi/

6 The four drivers of fitness-tech startups

How to build a survey

6.1 How to choose the sample

The research aims to focus on global startups for which information could be found without accessing specific databases. In fact, a first major obstacle to finding information is the lack of a comprehensive database that includes a reasonable number of startups from all continents. Since no specific database like this, or is publicly available, exists to date, its construction for the purpose of this research was deemed fundamental (Thompson. 2018).

To build the database, it was necessary to select startups according to four specific criteria in order to better contextualize the sample:

1 **Availability of a website**: Since the main topic hinges on undertakings that are closely connected to digital technology, the existence of a dedicated website was considered a "must-have". More specifically, this criterion stipulates the existence of a dedicated website as a minimum requirement since some of these initiatives also have a dedicated app within which digital content is posted. Therefore, a source without a dedicated website was not considered sufficiently reliable and was not included in the sample.
2 **Geographical area of origin**: Based on the origin of the undertaking, certain assessments need to be made. In particular, it was noted that there are many startups in this industry in the USA. American practice normally provides for a certain minimum of documentation, and media attention tends to be very high and receptive to these new initiatives, especially in the post-COVID period. Therefore, it was much easier to find news and data on American startups than for all other geographical areas. However, precisely because the intention was not to provide an outlook on only the, albeit vibrant, North American market but, rather, to give an overall view, it was decided to set an upper limit of max 50% on American undertakings. The remaining 50% of the sample had to include fitness-tech startups from other continents. In this second case, however, the ease of finding valuable and reliable sources decreased sharply. Thanks to essential contributions from influential newspapers, it was possible to successfully bridge the gap and also populate the remaining 50% of the database. Specifically, Europe

DOI: 10.4324/9781003475699-7

produced good results, as it proved to be a good compromise between the number of nascent businesses and the attention of information sources toward them. This mix of factors produced a good number of analyzed startups from this geographical area. As far as Asia-Pacific is concerned, as can be guessed, by far the largest number of fitness-tech startups in this region was registered in China. This acknowledgment prompted us to focus on the business initiatives that are spreading in the Land of the Red Dragon. Finally, with regard to the Middle East, the state of Israel appears to be the most prosperous in terms of business initiatives there. The information gap between the various areas of the world remains considerable, as during the information search activity, the difference between sources from North America, particularly the USA, compared to both Europe and Asia was evident. Ultimately, those countries that are demonstrating a growth path by leveraging increasingly receptive demand, a growing business environment, and a generally positive trend should also be mentioned. Although they do not have many startups to be analyzed; yet, both Brazil and India are most likely to see increases in the future.

3 **Primary focus on fitness**: Another criterion was the core of the activity identified. Whenever it was noted that the focus was on physical activity of any kind (for example, anything from weightlifting to yoga), the startup was deemed appropriate. Conversely, whenever the core business activity seemed to be directed toward nutrition rather than sleep or meditation, then its relevance to the purpose of the research was taken into further consideration. This was because, despite focusing on sports practices, the aim was not to scout for companies that specialize in competitive training for the preparation of professional athletes. On the contrary, the goal was to target all those young promising enterprises promoting a holistic approach to personal care and well-being. Therefore, startups that proved to offer sports activity for common people, or amateurs, as their primary mission were perfectly fitting. Meanwhile, those other startups focused on other related facets of wellness, like healthy food preparation and distribution, for example, or startups that offered courses on how to sleep effectively, were analyzed twice to better understand if their core business might fit with the scope of this research.

4 **Grade of notoriety matured over time**: The three criteria listed above are reasonably followed by a fourth, notoriety. This is important because the more promising a startup is, the more attention it receives in the media, including newspapers, magazines, and other mediums. Since greater media attention inevitably corresponds to a greater number of interviews, articles, and videos that bring a business story to light, this factor contributes to the number of entries on the web, which, in turn, connects with the ease of scouting by the web searcher. Therefore, the more "famous" a startup becomes, the more likely it is that it will be easy to find it and write about

it. Consequently, a lack of notoriety and, thus, of information that could be found on the web may have caused some startups to be left out of this analysis.

Following the four abovementioned criteria, the total sample of fitness-tech startups is exactly 100. In graphical terms, the total composition looks as follows (Figure 6.1):

As you can see, the most frequent geographical area is the Americas. This is due to the large number of publicly available information sources. As you will see in the next graph, this figure was influenced by the massive presence of North American companies compared to South American ones. However, the maximum limit of 50 startups from this geographical area was fully respected. Secondly, Europe has shown an important presence of entrepreneurial realities in this sector, as demonstrated by their frequency. As the next graph shows, in this second case, the origin is much more fragmented and divided among the major countries. Thirdly, the Asia-Pacific area has significantly fewer startups than the first two groups. This is mainly due to the lack of data related to companies in this sector that can be freely consulted from Italy. In any case, China makes up a large part of the total of this geographical area. Finally, the only startups detected in the Middle East region came from the state of Israel. There is no other info about companies from other countries in this region.

Going into even more detail, the graph below shows the breakdown of the startups identified for this study by country (Figure 6.2):

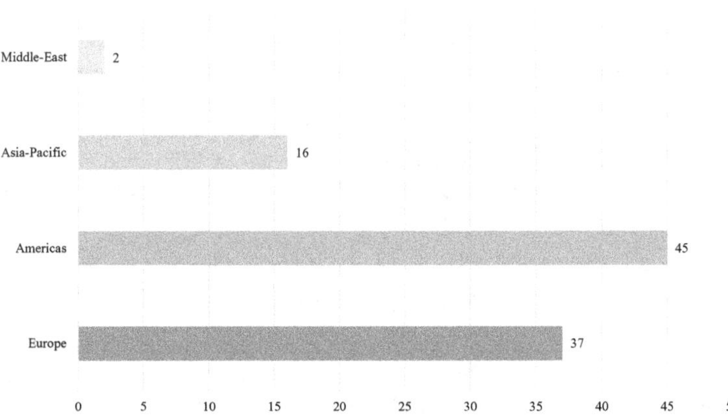

Figure 6.1 Fitness-tech startups breakdown by geographical area

Source: Own research

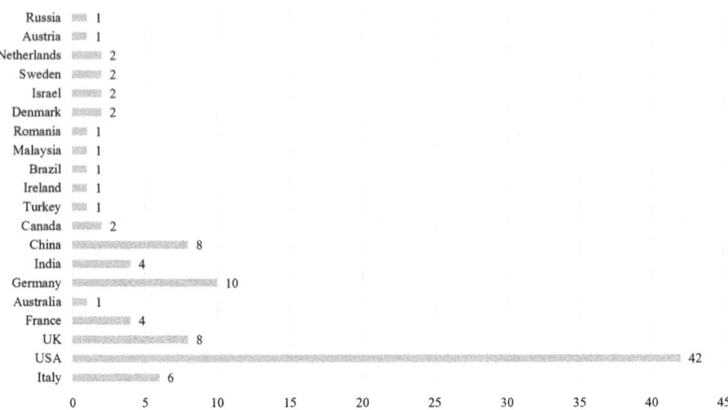

Figure 6.2 Fitness-tech startups breakdown by country

Source: Own research

In this second graph, the first reflection is that the USA have a far higher frequency (42) compared to any other country in the world. This is not a coincidence; it is the result of a strong interest in wellness and sport, as well as, and perhaps especially, a lively, young, and innovative entrepreneurial environment boasting huge flows of capital from both private investors and the financial markets. Several European countries are also prospering in this industry, with an interesting number of startups in the field. These include Germany (10), the UK (8), Italy (6), and France (4). As has already been said, Europe presents the most geographically fragmented landscape, but it is no less interesting because of that. Finally, the two most prosperous Asian countries in this industry are China (10) and India (4). Although they have not yet reached the numbers of Europe and America, given their economic growth and the social consequences that this will entail, it will certainly be very interesting to follow their course in the years to come.

6.2 Survey: structure and questions

After scouting for entrepreneurial initiatives in the fitness-tech field that are growing globally and conducting an initial screening according to the four criteria detailed above, we created a survey to further study the identified startups. The survey, entitled "Market Research: Fitness-tech Startups", is set up in six sections based on the four already-mentioned drivers plus introductory concluding sections. The title defines the business purpose of this analysis, without anticipating any particular findings, which will be highlighted later.

- Section 1 → **Intro**: The introductory section of the survey opens with a brief description and identifies the objectives the study aims to achieve. It then briefly mentions the four drivers addressed within the individual sections. It was particularly important to provide this introduction because, unlike a survey directed at individuals, when communicating directly with small-, medium-, or even large-sized companies, it is important to be precise in defining the object and purpose of the analysis. The company contacted generally wants to know the subject matter in detail right away, so the level of communication must necessarily be greater from the outset. The introductory message reads as follows:

  "Dear Sirs and Madams, the purpose of this academic research is to obtain reliable information from target companies in order to gather real and objective insights into the performance of fitness-tech startups worldwide. Four different themes will be shown in this research, respectively referring to:

  1 **Sustainability** projects undertaken by the company
  2 Degree of **technological digitization** present in the company's processes
  3 **Financial performance** and capital obtained from shareholders
  4 Type of **business model (BM)** adopted

  We would like to inform you that the data entered here will only be processed in aggregate and in full compliance with privacy regulations".

  The first of the two introductory questions asked about the geographical area within which the target startups conduct their business. Here, the choice is deliberately broad, asking them to segment by geographical region and not by individual country, so the possible answers are North America, Latin America, Europe, Asia, Oceania, and Africa. This first question, therefore, captures the perimeter.

  The second introductory question aims to identify the size of the startup in terms of employees. In fact, one of the benchmarks when talking about company size is precisely the number of employees. From this figure, one could also partially estimate what figures to expect in terms of financing because, as is obvious, the number of employees is often directly proportional to the amount of capital received by way of investment from the various financiers. Therefore, the first two questions define the target area and size of the startups considered.

- Section 2 → **Sustainability**: The purpose of Section 2 is to introduce the first driver, sustainability. The following definition was included to frame a concept that is broadly used in various academic and scientific papers and to inform the respondents of what we wanted them to focus on:

"A Sustainability Program contains all projects involving topics and milestones related to sustainability goals like reducing air pollution, water consumption, energy waste and creating value for surrounding communities, employees, and shareholders".

The first question is of a preliminary nature, simply asking whether or not the company has a sustainability program, such as an ad hoc in-house program (León-Quismondo et al., 2020).

The second question requires companies to identify which, of those proposed, are the greatest perceived problems. In order to avoid confusion and create consistency for the purposes of analysis, the idea was to offer the following plausible choices: (1) improving worker engagement (Mella & Gazzola, 2018); (2) sharing the value created by the company with the surrounding community (Laszlo, 2008); (3) using zero-impact objects or equipment to reduce pollution from the use of objects that are difficult to dispose of; (4) reducing energy and electricity consumption through a careful cost-saving policy; and (5) reducing environmental impacts in terms of air quality and overall industrial impact (Fiore et al., 2015). Of these five options, each respondent could only select their top two concerns, thus creating a scale intended identify which of these issues each company is prioritizing the most.

The third question introduces the component of monitoring the progress of these initiatives, to understand whether they are just good intentions or real projects. Monitoring is considered a key element to understand the progress of well-intentioned initiatives. This information can shed light the maturity of such projects, distinguishing good intentions from real, concrete actions (Arnocky et al., 2014).

This question is followed by a self-assessment of the results achieved, regardless of the metrics used to check project progress. The final question asks respondents to identify what they think they have achieved so far (Elkington, 2012). Again, the aim is to find out how a company perceives of its work in relation to this issue. For this question, respondents can select from the following five milestones that are closely related to the five problems listed in question two of this section: (1) improved happiness of workers (Casey & Sieber, 2016); (2) improved life standards of local community (Kramer & Porter, 2011); (3) improved recycling within the firm (Shah et al., 2010); (4) reduced water and energy consumption (Aghelinejad et al., 2018); and (5) reduced air pollution (Zhu & Lee, 2021).

- Section 3 → **Technology**: This third section deals with technology. Here again, the following definition of technology is provided in order to frame the term and inform respondents (Millington, 2017).

  "By technology we mean the IT equipment used within business processes, the degree of digitization of these processes, and the possible implementation of proprietary technologies".

The first question is about whether the company has created a dedicated app to share video content with consumers (Mhalla et al., 2020). The need for this question stemmed from the realization that in the past couple of year many influencers and fitness-related digital businesses have started to create and share content through the use of specific apps.

The next question straightforwardly asks if the business offers video content to their users. Here again, it is expected that most respondents will answer in the affirmative, given the increasing digital impact on value propositions. If the previous question is answered in the affirmative, the next question seeks to investigate the tool or tools most frequently used to create and bring media content to the target audience. Here, respondents can choose from three possibilities: (1) own smartphone; (2) basic equipment costing $2,000 or less; or (3) professional equipment costing more than $2,000. In this specific case, the figures are not arbitrary. On the contrary, they are the result of a market analysis that identified the costs of specific items considered indispensable for the creation of certain content. Therefore, the designated price range is not random; it represents the sum of costs for individual items that are part of regularly used IT equipment.

The last question in this section asks whether the startup has implemented a new proprietary technology for the dissemination of media content or is relying on an already existing technology (Nesheim, 2000). Here, it must be pointed out that an existing technology does not necessarily compromise revenues; there is no consistent link between revenues and proprietary technology. One may very well buy a license for a particularly high-performance software and leverage it to better offer content to users (Usman & Vanhaverbeke, 2017). This question, therefore, served to identify how important it is for a startup to go to market with a proprietary technology and, thus, with a particularly high level of technology (Pizzo et al., 2020).

- Section 4 → **Financing**: This fourth section deals with another very important topic, financing (Landier, 2003). It is regarded by some experts as the petrol that enables a startup to continue to travel along its path of business growth. In this brilliant metaphor, the various funding rounds are compared to the function performed by petrol pumps. Each funding round can be seen as a petrol pump where one can refuel during a journey. If a startup cannot find the next petrol pump, or if the amount of petrol is insufficient to cover the stretch of road between one petrol pump and the next, then that startup runs the risk of not being able to continue growing and comes to an abrupt halt, just like a car that has run out of petrol. Here, however, in order to make the language more appropriate for academic research, the following definition is provided:

  "By funding we mean the amount of capital a startup has obtained so far from investments made by third parties called shareholders. These sums of money should have been obtained partly as startup capital to support set-up costs and partly through various funding rounds".

The first question in this section collects information about the company's history by asking about the year it was founded. Meşter and Gavriluţ (2023) argue that there is a correlation between the date of foundation of unicorn startup companies and their valuation and field of activity.

The second question is crucial, as one cannot talk about funding without understanding what stage the startup is at currently. In fact, it stands to reason that the more funding rounds a startup can boast, the greater its likelihood of success, as it is assumed that as time goes by, the business will grow enough to continue to make itself attractive in the eyes of more and more financiers (Fuertes-Callén et al., 2022). As time and funding rounds go by, more and more important investors will approach the startup. As the numbers consequently increase, the startup's reputation will be increasingly lauded in industry events and magazines, so more and more journalists will talk about its progress, creating a success narrative (Klačmer Čalopa et al., 2014). Funding, the growth of the business, and the fame gained through the media are all intertwined and feed off each other. In this case, the five proposed choices that respondents can choose from are as follows: (1) the so-called "seed" stage (i.e., early on, when the startup is not yet even a seedling but still a seed that could germinate; (2) the A round that sanctions the actual startup phase within a financial environment that is considerably amplified compared to before (in this second case, it has been ascertained that the seed from before has sprouted into a seedling); (3) the B round; (4), the C round (the third and fourth choices depict the growth process of a seedling that is becoming larger and larger); and, (5) the D rounds D, which depicts a plant that has become a tree or a startup that has become a well-established business and is creating significant revenues.

The third question is a direct consequence of the previous one; it gets more specific by asking how much funding the startup has received. Again, the range taken into consideration is not random, but the result of an analysis carried out by the well-known consulting firm KPMG (Mincey & Collin, 2024), whose report provides clear data in this regard. After a careful analysis of those figures, we decided to create the numerical ranges proposed in the survey as a good approximation of the lower and upper extremes offered by KPMG. So, again, nothing is left to chance.

Finally, the last question in this section is intended to be even more technical. One of the most figures to know when talking to investors is the target figure you need to carry on your business for at least 1.5–2 years before needing further financing. If having too much cash can lead to an excessive squandering of resources, compromising the optimal management of the money obtained, having too little leads entrepreneurs to get trapped in fundraising activity, perpetually searching for new funds and unable to attend to the most important thing, i.e., the strategic planning and management of the business. Therefore, one must always strive for an optimal level of funding, neither too much nor too little. (Dimova, 2021) When you put a required amount of money on the table, you also include the percentage of equity that you are willing to grant to investors in order to obtain returns from your investment. Dividends and any interest charged thus constitute the investors' remuneration and their reason for investing in a certain business. When an entrepreneur knows the amount they need to carry on their business for a reasonable period of time, as well as the amount of equity they are willing to grant, then the post-money valuation can be calculated on the basis of these expectations. From the post-money, one can then obtain the pre-money, also based on the company's financing history. The pre-money valuation is required in order to exclude the expectation element and obtain "clean" numbers based only on the capital obtained so far that. The valuation, therefore, takes place before a financing round and describes a company's financial situation at an exact point in time. Again, the pre-money options were obtained not by selecting figures at random, but by referring to KPMG's (Mincey & Collin, 2024) report on the private equity world. While this report is certainly the basis for the numerical range explained in the survey, it is supplemented with the considerations and particularities of the case under consideration.

- Section 5 → **Business Model**: The penultimate section of this survey concerned the startups' primary BM. The following definition is provided to frame the term:

  "By business model we primarily mean the way in which the startup is able to generate revenues, but not only that. It also indicates a framework within which the company establishes relationships with suppliers and customers and manages its core activities".

  The first question in this section deals with the adoption of the BM and proposes five possible models. In this case, no explanation is given for each of them to avoid further burdening a survey that already contains important and time-consuming questions. Furthermore, all entrepreneurs in the fitness industry have a certain level of knowledge about their own BM in relation to others, as it is one of the first things to consider when deciding to start a business in this market. In fact, one of the first questions one usually faces is the debate about the most correct way to generate revenue, so it is reasonable to think that the people responding to this survey have already scouted the various eligible and convenient BMs and their degree of knowledge is not zero. For this reason, it seems superfluous to define every single BM proposed and, thereby, burden the survey unnecessarily (Addolorato et al., 2024). The five proposed BMs begin with a very "traditionalist" first choice, the Membership-based model that is used by all traditional fitness companies (Murray & Williams, 2021). It is the "classic" model, but also the most basic one. In contrast, the second is much more modern and in step with the times, as the Hybrid model combines both the classic Membership-based model and the online model developed by trainers, experts, or even amateurs who are passionate about a certain discipline. During the COVID pandemic, fitness and wellness content on the web exploded due to the general need to exercise while staying at home during lockdowns. Even in the post-COVID era, this digital content remains and has been consolidated, so there is a merging of the physical and digital training worlds. The online world has expanded the offerings of fitness centers by raising industry benchmarks even higher. The third model is the more "classic" franchise model, which existed long before COVID, but which still retains significance; in fact, the advantages associated with this BM remain considerable, so it is easy to understand why it is timeless. The penultimate model is the Digital subscription only model, which is based on the exclusive use of digital content. This BM literally exploded during COVID and led to the emergence of new stars, fitness influencers (Lawrence, 2022). While such figures, who acted as guides for so many enthusiasts, existed before COVID, many other personalities managed to emerge during the pandemic to take advantage of the radical change of environment. The fitness world within the wellness universe was called upon to change content, to improvise or innovate, depending on your perspective (Ziółkowska & Taraszkiewicz, 2022). The fact is that new personalities and new content have popped up, and the public seems to appreciate the versatility, practicality, and usefulness of this new content. Therefore, it should not be strange to see people deciding to train exclusively at home rather than attending a sports center. This is why an exclusively digital-based BM deserves special attention and to be mentioned as an option in its own right. Finally, the pay-as-you-go model is listed for completeness of options. In fact, such a model describes all those fitness and wellness experiences related to exclusivity, particularity, and the creation of a unique user experience that can adapt to the extreme dynamism often required by modern standards of living.

The penultimate question concerns the company's cost structure. Although it may seem peculiar, it is intended to address the assumption that many digitally based businesses have a much more variable cost structure than more "traditional", physically based businesses. The much lower set-up costs, shorter payback times, ease of getting out of an investment sooner and with less eventual loss, hiring and firing flexibility, and revenue-generating versatility are all potentially influential factors depending on whether one is talking about a variable or fixed cost structure.

Finally, the last question in the fourth section concerns customer retention (Yi et al., 2021). This data is a source of curiosity, as it could confirm or disprove the assumption that customer variability is also a factor in the context of digital business. Given the vast choice that exists within the various platforms online, the consumer is able to find similar services very easily, and given that the ease and speed of changing from one supplier to another is also high, it could be deduced that customer retention is not high for this type of business (Lee et al., 2021). Therefore, this question is intended to confirm or overturn the initial assumption and provide further insights.

- Section 6 → **Ending**: Following the five previous sections and four main drivers, the survey closes with an elegant and formal message that thanks the respondent for their time and reiterates the importance of spotlighting the fitness-tech startups market, which has undergone major upheavals in recent years.

  The survey ends by asking if the respondent would be interested in receiving updates on the insights gained from the study. If so, they must submit an email address in order to receive the document containing the final results of this research.

6.3 The survey: the form

The entire survey is shared below.

—

The purpose of this survey is to obtain reliable information from target companies in order to gather real and objective insights into the performance of fitness-tech startups worldwide. This survey covers the following four themes:

1 **Sustainability** projects undertaken by the company.
2 Degree of **technological digitization** present in the company's processes.
3 **Financial performance** and capital obtained from shareholders.
4 Type of **business model** adopted.

We would like to inform you that the data entered here will only be processed in aggregate and in full compliance with privacy regulations.

Intro
Where do you primarily do business?

- ○ North-America
- ○ Latin-America
- ○ Europe
- ○ Asia
- ○ Oceania
- ○ Africa

How many employees do you currently employ?

- 1
- 2–10
- 11–50
- 51–250

Sustainability
A Sustainability Program contains all projects involving topics and milestones related to sustainability goals like reducing air pollution, water consumption, energy waste and creating value for surrounding communities, employees, and shareholders.

Do you have a Sustainability Program?

- Yes
- No

What are your major challenges? (max. 2 choices)

- Improving employee engagement
- Sharing value with surrounding communities
- Using recyclable-only items/equipment
- Reducing water/energy consumption
- Reducing air pollution

Do you use any software/metric to monitor your sustainability progresses?

- Yes
- No

How is your commitment to sustainability going in terms of results?

- Just started
- Not so good
- Pretty good
- Very good

Your achievements so far have… (max. 2 choices)

- Improved the happiness of your employees
- Improved the life standards of your local community
- Improved recycling within the firm
- Reduced water/energy consumption
- Reduced air pollution

Technology
By technology we mean the IT equipment used within business processes, the degree of digitization of these processes, and the possible implementation of proprietary technologies.

Have you developed a dedicated app to bring your value proposition to the attention of your customers?

- Yes
- No

Do you offer online video content?

- Yes
- No

Which tools/devices do you regularly use to produce the video content you offer to your customers?

- Just a smartphone
- Basic equipment (max $2,000 total set-up costs)
- Professional equipment (more than $2,000 set-up costs)

Have you developed a new technology (IP, patent, software), or are you using an existing one to implement the video content platform you offer to your customers?

- New
- Existing

Financing

By funding we mean the amount of capital your startup has obtained so far through investments made by third parties called shareholders. These sums of money should have been obtained partly as start-up capital to support set-up costs and partly through various funding rounds.

When did you start your business?

- 10+ years ago
- 5–9 years ago
- 2–4 years ago
- 1 year or less

How many rounds of funding have you completed?

- Seed
- Series A
- Series B
- Series C
- Series D or more

How much capital have you raised so far? (in million dollars)

- $0–$2
- $3–$15
- $16–$35

- $36–$65
- $66–$100
- $100+

Your pre-money valuation? (in million dollars)

- Less than $5
- $5–$10
- $11–$50
- $51–$200
- $201–$400
- $400+

Business Model

By business model, we primarily mean the way in which the startup is able to generate revenue, but not only that. It also indicates a framework within which the company establishes relationships with suppliers/customers and manages its core activities.

Which of the following Business Models are closest to yours? (max. 2 choices)

- Membership-based
- Hybrid (membership + online classes)
- Franchising
- Digital subscription
- Pay-as-you-go

Your cost structure is mostly…

- Fixed
- Variable

Your customer retention is…

- Low
- Medium
- High

Ending

Thank you for your time!

The purpose of this survey is to spotlight the importance and growth of the fitness-tech industry.

Would you like to receive further updates about the results of this survey?

- Yes
- No

If Yes, please submit your email address.

—

References

Addolorato, S., Fernández, J. G., Guerrero, L. G., & Unanue, J. G. (2024). The fitness "working class" and its relationship with fitness equipment: a systematic review. *Retos: nuevas tendencias en educación física, deporte y recreación*, 51, 1318–1332.

Aghelinejad, M., Ouazene, Y., & Yalaoui, A. (2018). Production scheduling optimisation with machine state and time-dependent energy costs. *International Journal of Production Research*, *56*(16), 5558–5575.

Arnocky, S., Milfont, T. L., & Nicol, J. R. (2014). Time perspective and sustainable behavior: Evidence for the distinction between consideration of immediate and future consequences. *Environment and Behavior*, *46*(5), 556–582.

Casey, D., & Sieber, S. (2016). Employees, sustainability and motivation: Increasing employee engagement by addressing sustainability and corporate social responsibility. *Research in Hospitality Management*, *6*(1), 69–76.

Dimova, D. (2021). Investment attractiveness of wellness sector. *Предприемачество*, *9*(2), 47–57.

Elkington, J. (2012). *The zeronauts: Breaking the sustainability barrier*. Routledge, London.

Fiore, A. M., Naik, V., & Leibensperger, E. M. (2015). Air quality and climate connections. *Journal of the Air & Waste Management Association*, *65*(6), 645–685.

Fuertes-Callén, Y., Cuellar-Fernández, B., & Serrano-Cinca, C. (2022). Predicting startup survival using first years financial statements. *Journal of Small Business Management*, *60*(6), 1314–1350.

Klačmer Čalopa, M., Horvat, J., & Lalić, M. (2014). Analysis of financing sources for start-up companies. *Management: Journal of Contemporary Management Issues*, *19*(2), 19–44.

Kramer, M. R., & Porter, M. (2011). *Creating shared value* (Vol. 17). Boston, MA: FSG.

Landier, A. (2003). Start-up financing: From banks to venture capital. Unpublished working paper. University of Chicago, Chicago, IL.

Laszlo, C. (2008). *Sustainable value: How the world's leading companies are doing well by doing good*. Stanford University Press, Stanford.

Lawrence, S. (Ed.). (2022). *Digital wellness, health and fitness influencers: Critical perspectives on digital guru media*. Taylor & Francis, New York.

León-Quismondo, J., García-Unanue, J., & Burillo, P. (2020). Best practices for fitness center business sustainability: A qualitative vision. *Sustainability*, *12*(12), 5067.

Mella, P., & Gazzola, P. (2018). Corporate social responsibility through stakeholder engagement and entrepreneurial communication processes. *International Journal of Business Performance Management*, *19*(1), 36–54.

Meşter, i., & Gavriluţ, d. (2023). The secrets of Unicorn companies: An empirical investigation. *The Annals of the University of Oradea*, *32*(1st), 205.

Mhalla, M., Yun, J., & Nasiri, A. (2020). Video-sharing apps business models: TikTok case study. *International Journal of Innovation and Technology Management*, *17*(07), 2050050.

Millington, B. (2017). *Fitness, technology and society: Amusing ourselves to life*. Routledge, London.

Mincey, G., & Collin, J. (2024). A better rebuild: Private Equity in the new reality. KPMG. Available at the following link: https://kpmg.com/xx/en/home/insights/2021/03/a-better-rebuild-private-equity-in-the-new-reality.html

Murray, D., & Williams, K. (2021). The Australian fitness industry: Trends, disruption and positioning. In *The global private health & fitness business: A marketing perspective* (pp. 111–117). Emerald Publishing Limited, Leeds.

Nesheim, J. L. (2000). *High tech start up, revised and updated: The complete handbook for creating successful new high tech companies*. New York: Simon and Schuster.

Pizzo, A. D., Baker, B. J., Jones, G. J., & Funk, D. C. (2020). Sport experience design: Wearable fitness technology in the health and fitness industry. *Journal of Sport Management, 35*(2), 130–143.

Shah, P., Gosavi, A., & Nagi, R. (2010). A machine learning approach to optimise the usage of recycled material in a remanufacturing environment. *International Journal of Production Research, 48*(4), 933–955.

Thompson, W. R. (2018). Worldwide survey of fitness trends for 2019. *ACSM's Health & Fitness Journal, 22*(6), 10–17.

Usman, M., & Vanhaverbeke, W. (2017). How start-ups successfully organize and manage open innovation with large companies. *European Journal of Innovation Management, 20*(1), 171–186.

Yi, S., Lee, Y. W., Connerton, T., & Park, C. Y. (2021). Should I stay or should I go? Visit frequency as fitness centre retention strategy. *Managing Sport and Leisure, 26*(4), 268–286.

Zhu, C., & Lee, C. C. (2021). The internal and external effects of air pollution on innovation in China. *Environmental Science and Pollution Research, 28*(8), 9462–9474.

Ziółkowska, J., & Taraszkiewicz, T. (2022). Changing business models-how fitness centers reacted to COVID-19: the case study of a Polish fitness operator. In *Research Handbook on Sport and COVID-19* (pp. 55–66). Edward Elgar Publishing. Northampton

7 The fitness-tech landscape

How do these startups behave?

7.1 Introduction

The fitness market is not a low-tech market. Sport is no longer primarily focused on performance. These two statements may seem strange, a little too brave, but they represent exactly what is happening. They represent change. Regarding the first statement, this research will show the surprising results regarding this sector's new entrepreneurial realities, which are increasingly tech-intensive. The massive presence of this technological component, and its influence on other drivers, has led us to talk specifically about "fitness tech" startups. Today's more "traditional" startups are still embracing the wave of digitalization that is flooding all sectors, while the most pioneering are reinventing fitness. The need to reinvent this practice lies in the generalized tendency to see sport less and less as aimed at a competition, and increasingly as a necessary practice for one's own psycho-physical well-being. A fitness of all, for all. Thus, digital and technological innovations are being used to bring fitness into consumers' homes, to make it as practical and useful as possible. This research aims to provide evidence of this shift, highlighting the young and dynamic world of fitness-tech startups.

7.2 Research methodology

First, it was necessary to carry out a scout analysis in order to collect all the information available about the sample we intended to build. As already explained in the previous chapters, it was much easier to get results for some countries, while the research was more time- and energy-intensive for others. The factors contributing this to difference are many, but they include the incidence of the total number of startups in a certain country or geographical area, the availability of information media, the availability of free online resources, the compatibility of some websites with the security policies of the search engines used, and technological constraints of various kinds. Nevertheless, in order not to create an excessively unbalanced and unrepresentative sample, we decided to set numerical thresholds above which it was not possible to

DOI: 10.4324/9781003475699-8

proceed. This led to the selection of startups from various regions of the world and made this research global in scope. The total number of the sample, 100, was chosen arbitrarily following two main assumptions:

1 The absence of previous research analyzing such a high number of startups under the profile of the four drivers identified, which were discussed in previous chapters. Although there are market studies with a much higher number of objects in the sample, these are usually based on existing, structured databases and conclusions of other authors. By adding an extra insight, it is possible to create a progression in the search field. Even at the data level, information can be taken from existing databases, blended, cleansed, filtered, and then aggregated according to a specific purpose. In this case, instead, there was a total absence of structured databases containing the list of startups that were the object of this analysis. This made the work of collecting information much more time-consuming and burdensome. When accounting for the cleaning and selection work that was done during the scouting phase, the number of objects examined was much greater than the 100 units selected.
2 The right balance between a sufficiently large number of startups and the quality standards in the selection of the same. In fact, while a small number could have ensured greater filtering and, therefore, an even more accurate targeting of entrepreneurial realities in fitness-tech, we tried to reach the maximum possible number of startups to have an important sample in numerical terms. Hence, 100 was the most feasible.

With the goal of providing insightful information on the fitness-tech market with a focus on the four economic drivers of sustainability, technology, financing, and business model (BM), the analysis of these factors and their essential characteristics was carried out in the following manner:

Step 1 → Identification and selection of the sample

This first step describes how we identified and selected the startups considered in this research. Without wishing to mention the names of the companies taken into consideration for privacy reasons, we can and must, however, mention the selection criteria adopted during the scouting phase to understand their eligibility and their adherence to the following criteria:

- Availability of a website
- Geographical area of origin
- Primary focus on fitness
- Grade of notoriety matured over time

Step 2 → Creating a database

After checking each startup by studying each website repeatedly in order to best understand its message and, more specifically, what the company wants to convey through its main "showroom", we went about creating a database. Therefore, an Excel sheet was created containing all the information with the most important characteristics of the companies examined. In particular, the following publicly obtainable information was collected:

- Name
- Website
- Email address
- Country of origin
- Level of sustainability
- Technological advancement
- Funding—Inception date
- Funding—Number of rounds
- Funding—Type of round
- Funding—Total amount obtained so far
- Business model

Step 3 → Assessment of sustainability

Considering the terminological framework of what can be defined by "sustainability", as expressed in Chapter 6, we then proceeded to set the criteria for understanding how important this driver is and how that importance is communicated by each startup. In particular, a tripartition was set out as follows:

- Highly present
- Just mentioned
- Not shown

The term "*highly present*" was used to refer to all those startups that care about sustainability and convey it with the utmost care on the home page of their website. They use their online presence to showcase their attention to this issue, including their sensitivity and their receptiveness to undertake pioneering initiatives in order to preserve their principles. Hence, it describes the startups that are most attentive and best able to communicate this attention right from the home page of their website, meaning that there is no need to scroll down or wander around the website to see any reference to this theme. Thus, identification of sustainability as "*highly present*" in a company indicates that from a first glance at the website, one can see unmistakable evidence of their emphasis related to this theme. Initiatives, projects, and ambitions were described, or at the very least, sustainability was mentioned as an issue that the company was going to improve through its product/service.

The term "*just mentioned*", however, was used to refer to all those startups that, although they did not show the greatest attention to this issue, nevertheless uploaded blog articles to their site or communicated about projects related to it. Here, communication took place at a lower level, as there was no reference to sustainability on the home page, but if one reads the blog or scrolls down the site, they can still discover some elements related to it. This was a sign not only of attention but also of present and sufficient communication, although it could certainly be improved. If the companies themselves have not found it essential to better communicate their sustainability efforts to date, one hypothesis might be that it is not important to them, or if it is important, due attention has not been paid to better communication of its importance. Therefore, "*just mentioned*" indicates that some elements or hints of sustainability have been found, but the communication could be improved.

Lastly, the term "*not shown*" represents all those startups that do not mention any initiative, project, or stimulus toward sustainability on their website. It should be noted at this point that we are not claiming that these companies are not sensitive to this issue; in fact, many of them may be very adherent to the principles of sustainability and are striving to spread the right culture of work as a place to create value and share it with the surrounding community. Therefore, this is not to say that all companies that have been labeled as "*not shown*" are against these dictates or indifferent to this issue. What is meant, instead, is that they have clearly not paid attention to communication. They have not considered it important to communicate their efforts, if any, in this regard. They have decided to direct their communication exclusively to the product, its features and functionality, the problems it solves, and the consumers it addresses, without mentioning the principles of sustainability. This is not intended as a necessarily negative judgment of them. We just want to bring a fact to light, hopefully as an impulse for improvement.

Step 4 → Assessment of technology

The focus of the discourse in this context revolves around the company's IT systems and the possible implementation of proprietary technologies of some value. It was decided to divide the degree of technology detected into these categories:

- Radical
- Incremental
- Standard

"*Radical*" technology is precisely that with the highest rate of technological value, not just the improvement of an existing object or process, but the design and engineering of something new that often revolutionizes the very concept of fitness or the realization of something that the consumer could not see coming. Within this prestigious category, therefore, are only those startups that have created something extraordinarily innovative, shocking the market with their technological potential and impressing both consumers by filling them with awe and the players currently in the market by pushing the benchmark even higher. We usually think of well-established companies as the initiators of more radical innovations, but this thinking is wrong. There are startups that have proven that they can also bring out state-of-the-art technologies and surprise everyone.

The second category identified was "*incremental*" technologies, i.e., improvements to existing objects or software. Here, nothing particularly innovative or disruptive that would impress consumers or competitors is created, but improvements are made to something that already exists. Examples might include a particularly successful piece of software that is able to improve, by a great deal, the performance of an older one taken as a reference model or a piece of gym equipment that has been made more ergonomic, functional, and practical as a result of innovative advances. Although there is nothing ground-breaking, these changes can be identified as improvements because consumers come to appreciate them a lot, which usually leads to an increase in sales. Therefore, sometimes an improvement is enough to make a startup a success compared to its competitors. One does not need to invent the moon to be perceived as better by customers.

Finally, the last category concerned existing technologies defined as "*standard*" in that they are already on the market, adopted by a more or less long series of companies, each with its own particularities. At the level of technology, therefore, we are not talking about anything exciting or new but, rather, something already seen elsewhere that can be better applied and still bear fruit. The technological component does not necessarily have to be the workhorse of a startup. In fact, innovation can also come from a non-technological novelty, but the purpose here was to perform a deep dive on the tech side.

Step 5 → Assessment of financing

The third driver discussed in this section is related to the financial aspect of the startups under consideration, in particular the aspect most keenly felt by them, namely the ability to attract funding from different types of investors, from friends and family to private equity funds and so on. In this case, given the heterogeneity of the situation, it was not possible to simplify the rationale into three levels. Therefore, we limited ourselves to reporting the number of funding rounds that the startups under investigation engaged in prior to the tracking date, the type of rounds the startups had access to prior to the tracking date, and the amount of capital obtained. In particular, the amount recorded was reported in USD as the reference currency for several reasons. First, many startups come from Anglo-American geographical areas, where the prevailing currency is the US dollar. Therefore, even if the information obtained was found in other currencies, it was converted into USD according to the conversion rate applied by the market at the time of the survey. Second, reporting the values in a single reference currency was a methodological requirement, as we wanted to give a homogeneous idea of the various amounts obtained from the different companies in order to make reading and understanding any comparisons between them as clear as possible. Depending on the degree of development and importance of the startups in the various markets within the different countries, the number of funding rounds, nomenclature, and corresponding amounts change considerably. Therefore, it should not be surprising if the final amounts are also significantly different for the same number of funding rounds or the same type of round. Finally, it should be pointed out that the time of observation was January 2024.

Step 6 → Assessment of business model

This last section deals with the methodology used to ascertain which BM startups were using at the time of the observation. In this case, it was possible to identify five different BMs in use among the sample companies:

- Membership-based
- Digital subscription
- Sale of product
- Hybrid (product + online contents)
- Pay-as-you-go

These five models were not chosen at random; they are the result of observations and comparisons after viewing their respective sites several times to understand what each startup offers and how it plans to generate revenue and capture value from its consumers.

The above-mentioned clusters were identified in the startups used in the sample. In particular, the geographical breakdown was as follows: 45% of the sample came from the Americas, 37% came from European countries, 16% came from the Asia-Pacific region, and only 2% came from the Middle East.

7.3 Main results

A first noteworthy fact concerns sustainability. It was found that 54% of the startups in our sample did not show any significant sign of sustainability efforts on their website. This does not necessarily mean that there are no sustainable companies at the organizational level; rather, it means that there is not communication about this effort where it is present. Therefore, there is much room for improvement from at least a communicative point of view. Only 30% show their commitment to sustainability on their website, either in a blog or scattered throughout different sections. Finally, only 16% of the sample immediately transmits, on the homepage, its interest in sustainability (Figure 7.1). We believe that this aspect of communication is also important, given the public's growing interest in this issue and the growing awareness of consumers.

As for the driver of technology shown in Figure 7.2, there was a generalized advance of the technological component in these new businesses. In fact, only 38% offered a product/service with a technological rate deemed standard. The remaining 62% showed an interesting progression compared to the past. Of the sample, 39% represent startups that are technologically

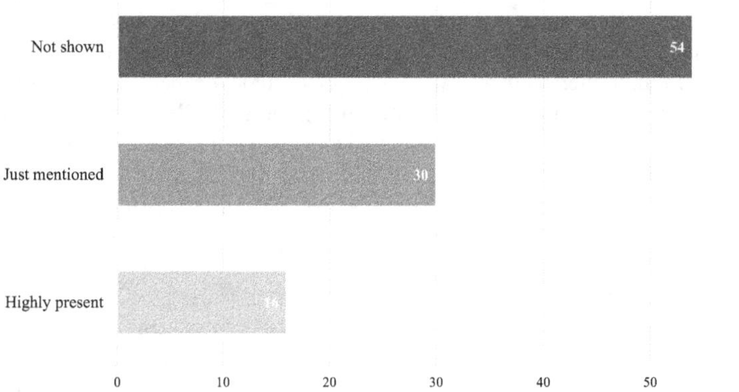

Figure 7.1 Sustainability efforts

Source: Own source with own edits

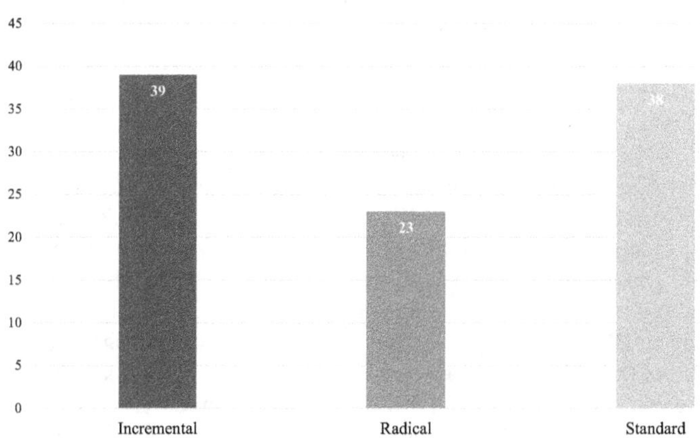

Figure 7.2 Types of technological advancement

Source: Own source with own edits

improving something already existing and, therefore, are innovating within their target market. Finally, 23%, so almost 1/4 of the total, are developing very advanced technologies compared to the standard level. As an example, what has been considered standard represents the products/services that we are used to thinking of when talking about sports, such as attending a yoga class. Thus, it has no negative meaning. It just represents things that we have already experienced. Instead, if we imagine doing yoga from the comfort of our home by following the instructions of a finely developed app that uses a high resolution to show the correct execution and give some suggestions, this represents an increase in technology. Finally, if we imagine a mat made with a "smart" fabric capable of detecting a series of biometric parameters useful to our health, immersed in a totally virtual environment capable of recreating the harmony of Koyasan in Japan, for example, this radically changes the way we conceive of practicing yoga compared to what we consider conventional.

A noteworthy correlation connects the startups' technological sphere with their BM. As shown in the third graph below, 78% of the startups that have been shown to have a high technological rate by implementing technologies classified as radical adopt an unconventional BM type. That is, they are not limited to the mere sale of their product but complement the offer with a range of ancillary services that are closely related to the main product. For example, in addition to offering a "smart mirror" that is able to act as a real virtual coach, correcting the performance of exercises, giving advice, etc., the famous startup Mirror, now part of the Lululemon universe, also offers a range of digital content that is relevant and useful in improving the overall user experience. It is a kind of sale of complementary products. In high-tech companies that develop technologically sophisticated products, the hardware is enriched by a very sophisticated software-side offer. Therefore, a BM that only includes the mere sale of products is not a wide enough framework to contain all the nuances of these firms, which is why their BM must be deemed as hybrid (Figure 7.3).

The chart below represents the frequencies detected for each of the BMs considered (Figure 7.4). As is evident, the highest frequency was detected for digital subscriptions (32%), which shows how the face of this sector is changing. In fact, the fitness market and the wellness industry, more generally, are opening up to digital, and one of the most evident signs of this opening is the change in the way these young companies do business. The second most frequent BM is hybrid (28%). This is also a very positive sign because it reflects the technological advancement of fitness-tech startups and the increasing complexity in the way they do business. The third most frequent is the sale of the product (23%), which proves to be evergreen. Finally, the last two BMs are pay-as-you-go (15%) and membership (2%) should not surprise, as they reflect, in the first case, an offer being spread among potential clients (think of the well-known case of Gympass) or, in the second case, an already mature and unappealing offer.

Given that the highest frequency detected between the various BMs was the digital subscription, it seemed appropriate to provide further information

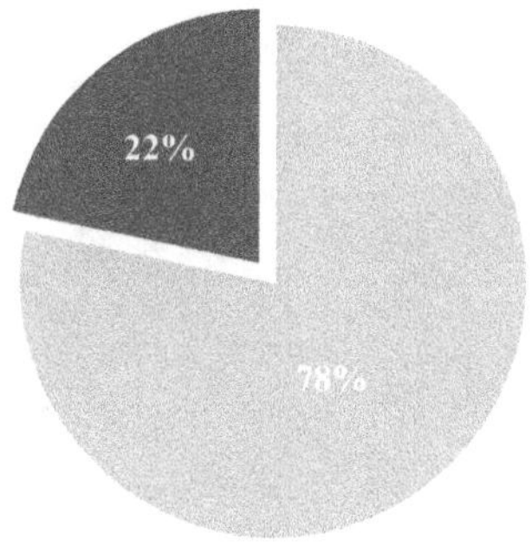

Figure 7.3 Business models adopted by those companies implementing radical technologies

Source: Own source with own edits

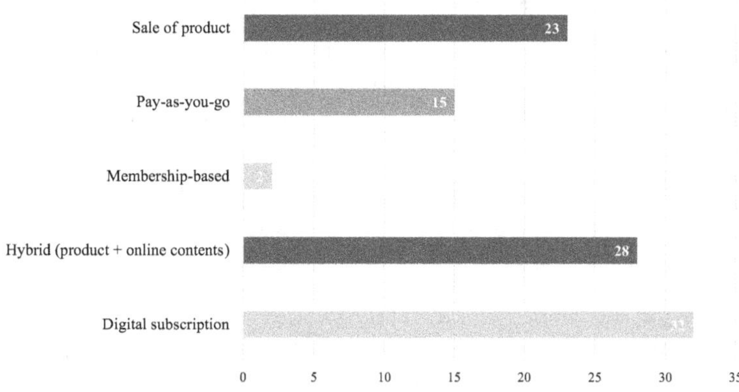

Figure 7.4 Types and frequencies of the identified business models

Source: Own source with own edits

about it (Figure 7.5). As the following pie chart shows, 66% of those who rely on subscriptions have a standard technology rate, while only a relative few (34%) bring a significant advancement in technology. As an example, we can think of those companies that develop software for other client companies. The technological layer is the same but used for different products and different customers. The technological layer does not necessarily have to be advanced to make companies profitable, as other factors also affect profit (for example, an efficient marketing campaign or the endorsement of famous influencers).

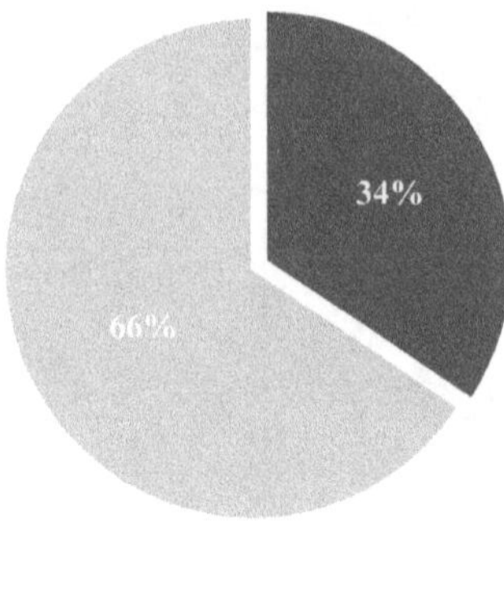

Figure 7.5 Technological rate for those startups adopting digital subscription as BM

Source: Own source with own edits

Another interesting data point shown below relates to the year that the startups in the sample were founded (Figure 7.6). The reference period runs from 2005 to 2020 and follows an interesting trend. Indeed, with a four-year transition from 2005, it can be seen that the number of enterprises is following an increasing trend. The largest increase was in the period 2013–2016, with 31 companies taken over, compared to 16 in the previous period. This figure may indicate that the innovative thrust of this sector dates back to before the pandemic and that COVID has done nothing but continue to accentuate gains in this area. The urgency to create something new had already been felt, so a growing number of startups were already "tech born". Finally, we want to note that the year of foundation was determined from the database on Crunchbase's website.

Crunchbase also collected an indication of the type of funding round that each startup had experienced at the time of the observation. Here, we have two macro-categories: the first group, representing 33% of the sample, are heterogeneous and have few standardizable indications (Other and Unknown), while the second group, representing 67% of the sample, includes those companies with information related to the most common and, therefore, known rounds (from Pre-Seed to round F). It can be noted that the first three frequencies detected are related to the Seed (15 units), A (21 units), and B (13 units) rounds, far greater than the others (Figure 7.7). This also underlines that we are talking about young, relatively recent startups that are, therefore, not very mature even from a financial point of view.

Finally, we want to provide a different representation of the data already mentioned and related to the types of funding. The funnel mechanism shows

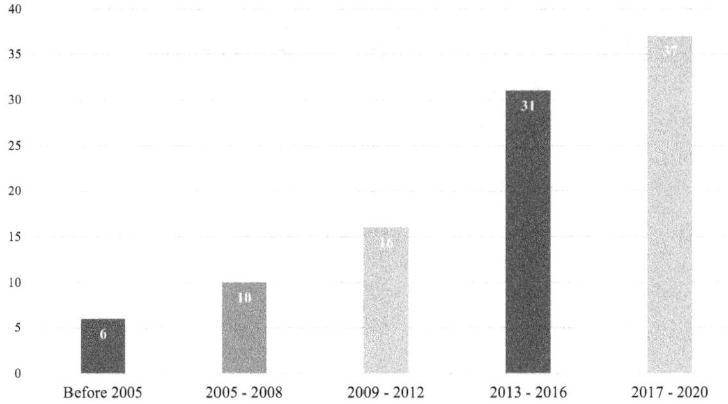

Figure 7.6 Foundation time range

Source: Own source with own edits

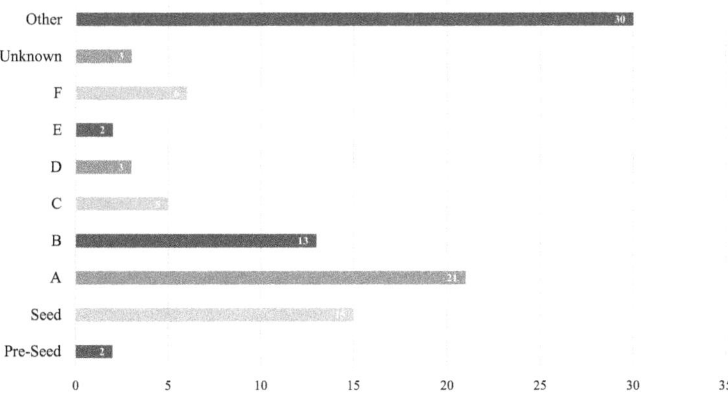

Figure 7.7 Types of funding rounds

Source: Own source with own edits

the progression of the frequencies detected, which are numerically consistent with what is usually expressed by the theory. As the funding rounds follow each other and the amount of money raised increases, the number of startups is naturally reduced compared to the total initial number (Figure 7.8). This is because the failure rate of these entrepreneurial realities is high and the chances of running out of cash during their journey and, thus, failing are always around the corner.

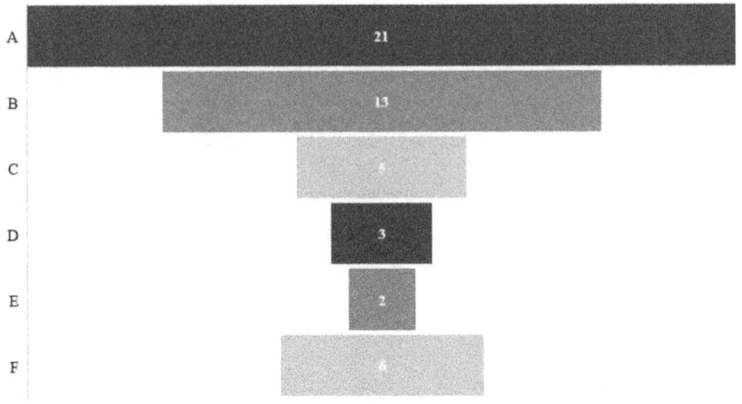

Figure 7.8 Funnel mechanism for the most common types of funding

Source: Own source with own edits

Conclusion

Fitness is part of the more general sector of so-called wellness, which is now a leading global sector on both the demand and supply sides. The increase in consumer spending power and a growing focus on personal care and well-being in the broadest sense, a trend that has accelerated since the COVID pandemic, have led to an exponential increase in demand, especially in the most advanced countries. The most recent studies show that the consumer is fundamentally influenced by drivers that seem destined to take on an increasing weight in the fitness sector: the growing consumption of natural and sustainable products, the search for personalized services, the importance of digitalization, and the influence of social media and influencers.

On the supply side, the sector looks extremely promising in terms of global development. Therefore, it is interesting to analyze the drivers that are responsible for the growth of fitness companies. First, the importance of what we have defined "traditional drivers" stands out, i.e., the financing and search for an adequate business model are essential conditions for the success of a company operating in the fitness sector, especially if it is a startup. In recent years, however, sustainability and innovation have driven the industry's evolutionary trajectory.

Second, it is well known how much consumer awareness of sustainability has increased over the years. In the same way, from a supply chain point of view, creating a sustainable business means ensuring the survival of the business in the long run. In the world of wellness, it is the social pillar of sustainability that takes on particular relevance, as evidenced by the development of the so-called Silver Economy, which can be considered as belonging to the sphere of wellness and which today appears to be on the rise, given the aging trend of the world population, especially in rich countries. Finally, the growing importance of the technological component within companies involved in the fitness sector stands out. Increased attention to the connectivity of devices, machinery, and any object used in sports at both professional and amateur levels is due to a change in trends on the part of consumers. This opens the door to interesting new business opportunities for operators in the sector.

DOI: 10.4324/9781003475699-9

The emerging global trends in the world of fitness are confirmed by the empirical survey carried out with 100 fitness-tech startups. The evidence that has emerged highlights a sector in strong turmoil, one that is experiencing an unprecedented fusion between technological implementation and marketing mix variables. The economic success of these companies is not only determined by their level of technological advancement, but also by their ability to expertly combine a mix of factors that can be purchasing drivers for potential consumers. In fact, it has also been found that current technological implementation diversified, composed both of companies capable of implementing cutting-edge technologies and companies that rely on pre-existing software or platforms to carry out their business. However, the decisive advantage of more tech-oriented companies is their ability to monitor the training and health status of their customers, collect and analyze the data in their possession, and possibly exploit it to implement new features aimed at customer satisfaction. Therefore, the ability to have control over data can lead these companies to develop a significant competitive advantage in the medium to long term.

Index

Note: *Italic* page numbers refer to figures.

For Product Safety Concerns and Information please contact our EU representative GPSR@taylorandfrancis.com
Taylor & Francis Verlag GmbH, Kaufingerstraße 24, 80331 München, Germany

www.ingramcontent.com/pod-product-compliance
Lightning Source LLC
LaVergne TN
LVHW010934110826
845149LV00013B/2598

* 9 7 8 1 0 3 2 7 5 7 9 3 3 *